AMERICA
AT WAR

The Battle for the Future of Our Nation

Johnny J. Esposito

PACIFIC PUBLICATIONS

2474 Pacific Avenue, Long Beach, California 90806

Phone (562) 424-7724   Fax (562) 424-3324

America at War: The Battle for the Future of Our Nation is dedicated to **Dr. Jack Hyles** for the great influence he had in my life and ministry, as well as the influence he has had throughout this nation and the world, and above all, to the Lord Jesus Christ who saved me from the depths of sin.

Copyright 2002 © by Johnny Esposito

Pacific Publications

All Rights Reserved

Printed in the United States of America by

Prestige Press, Inc. of North Little Rock, Arkansas 72117

Cover Design by Joseph Ledwidge & Margie Hawk

DISCLAIMER:

ISBN: 0-9715521-1-8

TABLE OF CONTENTS

ACKNOWLEDGMENTS

My first act of gratitude must be reserved for the Lord Jesus Christ who saved me and has sustained me for nearly 25 years now. The tremendous debt that I owe to my family, friends and mentors, is more than can ever be repaid. Whatever modest accomplishments have come my way including this book, are the result of the influence and inspiration of many. May the Lord Jesus Christ bless and reward each of them for the part they have played in my life and ministry.

After Christ, there have been many who have "helped me along the way." Of course, I would be remiss to not mention Denise, the love of my life, and my helpmeet for over twenty years now. I am thankful for a mother (Margaret Barnes) who loved me, an aunt (Annie Ryan) who acted as a second mother while I was a student in college. Thank God for a brother, my pastor, Dr. Joseph Esposito, who allowed me the privilege to work at the great Pacific Baptist Church.

Dr. Jack Hyles, for whom this book is dedicated, for his devotion to Christ and America – the land that he loved. Dr. Hyles helped me to become what I am today. Dr. Paul Chappell and Dr. Jack Trieber have not only been friends, but mentors. Their ministries, along with their manner of life have been a tremendous inspiration to me. These men, along with Dr. Eric Capaci, Dr. Mark Rasmussen, Dr. Lonnie Mattingly, Dr. Mark Turner, Dr. Darrell Moore, Pastor A.D. Hampton, and Pastor Randy Tewell in giving of their precious time to review this book, have been an incredible blessing, and for this I am grateful.

Special mention must be made for Dr. Mark Rasmussen and his wife Suza, my niece Taryn Ramirez, and my sister-n-law Mary Esposito for proofreading and editing this book. I thank God for America and the freedoms with which we have been blessed. May I do my part to pass on those freedoms to my five children (Jeremy, Joshua, John Nick, Jessica, & Joy) whom I love with all of my heart.

FOREWORD

Johnny Esposito is a man who labors in the education field, not merely in the academic arena, but also in the spiritual arena. This book, *America at War*, describes more than a philosophical battle-taking place in America today, including on our "public" school campuses. *America at War* describes the spiritual warfare, as well.

In the following pages, you will see from where America has come and where we are headed, as a nation, unless we see the kind of spiritual revival that would bring the needed changes to this nation.

This book will be a tremendous resource for pastors and educators seeking resource material on the current trends in our nation, especially on our school campuses. No doubt, the average lay person; especially parents will be greatly burdened and challenged by this book, as well.

In the closing chapter, "It's Time to Fight," the author challenges us to fight for what is good and right. America is truly at a crossroads right now. It is time for Christians to recognize that we must rise up and stand for what is right and holy. It is my prayer that this book will instruct and then inspire us to be valiant in the battle.

Dr. Paul Chappell

Pastor, Lancaster Baptist Church

President & Founder, West Coast Baptist College, Lancaster, CA

A WORD FROM OUR FRIENDS

Dr. Jack Trieber

As we enter the twenty-first century, it is clear that our beloved America is a nation deeply divided between those who hold to our Christian heritage and those who have given their loyalty to a secularized America that seeks to operate as though God does not exist. Brother Esposito is right. **America is at war**, and this ideological battle becomes increasingly fierce with the passing of each day. I believe that *America at War: The Battle for the Future of Our Nation* is a thought-provoking book that every sensitive Christian should read.

Pastor, North Valley Baptist Church
President & Founder, Golden State Baptist College, Santa Clara, CA

Dr. Lonnie Mattingly

I found this book by Johnny Esposito, **America at War**, to be captivating. It is aimed at the heart of the problem that we are facing in America today and it is right on target. Brother Esposito has done his homework. The research has been done and the documentation is superb. The author has gathered into one fact filled book enough compelling evidence to convince any sincere Christian that we are at war and the survival of our nation is at risk. In addition, the author gives us a call to Spiritual arms that should motivate us to positive action.

As in his previous book, *Temples of Darkness*, Johnny Esposito has proven to be a hard working "Blue Collar Scholar." I highly recommend this book. I will stock it in our bookstore and promote it from the Pulpit. It will become a textbook and a resource for our young people in the Christian School and Bible College.

Pastor, Shawnee Baptist Church
President & Founder Shawnee Baptist College, Louisville, Kentucky

Dr. Joseph Esposito

On the morning of September 11, 2001, the United States of America was awakened to a very fearful truth (that previously fell on deaf ears from so-called extremists) that "America Was at War." It took the lives of 3031 people to get our attention. Immediately our president said, "America is at war!" We spent billions of dollars in the first year of the war. The tragedy is that because we did not know that we were at war, we lost so many innocent lives.

My desire would be that this book would be to Christians, what September 11, 2001 was to America; a wake up call to enter the battle that we've been in for some time. May God use this book to help prevent the tragedy of losing our country to the Humanists, Atheists, Homosexuals and the ungodly enemies that have waged war on our Christian nation.

My brother, Johnny Esposito, has done a great job in his research to help us as God's people to understand that "We are at war." If we don't get in the fight, our country will soon be gone.

Pastor, Pacific Baptist Church, Long Beach, CA

Pastor A.D. Hampton

After reviewing the manuscript for the book, *America at War*, I was thankful for Brother Esposito's courage to put into print his convictions. As I read the manuscript, my heart rejoiced that this book would be published. At the same time, my blood began to boil because I am an American, and I love this country of ours. I spent 20 years in the Marine Corps defending the liberty and freedoms we enjoy in America, but due to some select groups, and their influence, our nation is no longer "One Nation Under God."

I believe that if this book would get into the hands of preachers across this nation, into Bible colleges, the Christian schools—if it could be taught to our young people, especially our young men preparing for the ministry—it would inspire them to have the courage to stand for what is right. I believe this *America at War* could be a tremendous help to our nation. I thank God for men like Brother Esposito who have the courage and convictions that are needed as we stand for righteousness and God. It indeed is time to fight. May we always proclaim the Word of God in power.

Barstow Baptist Temple, Barstow, CA

Pastor Randy Tewell

America at War is a call to spiritual arms for every God fearing American by a true Patriot. In this world of lukewarm Christianity and uncertain preaching, Brother Esposito gives a clarion call to each of us to join the battle to stem the tide of Communist philosophies, immoral activities, and the exclusion of God in our country. *America at War* is also an American history primer to remind us of the history and origin of our great nation and to remind us that in knowing that history, we can change the future. May God use this book to inspire thousands to fight the battle to win back the title "A Christian Nation" for our country.

Lighthouse Baptist Church, Theodore, Alabama

Dr. Mark Turner

In the battle for the morals of our nation, it is finally good to see a fundamental writer write on that which reflects upon the fundamental values that built America and made it great.

Pastor, Foothill Baptist Church, Moreno Valley, CA

Dr. Mark Rasmussen

America continues today to fight the war against terrorism. But there has been another war that has gone on far longer than this war on terrorism. This is the war many call the holy war. Brother Esposito delineates where the battle lines are drawn, he shows us who the enemy is, and he tells us what we can do to help win this war.

It is my opinion that full-time Christian workers across America would be well served by reading this book. While it is true that this book at times may shock, it is also true that this book should awaken those who take the time to read it. I, for one, am grateful for the diligent research and excellent writing that has helped me to become more aware of the spirit of America today.

Vice-President, West Coast Baptist College, Lancaster, CA

Dr. Eric Capaci

Once again, Brother Esposito has accomplished the task of providing valuable information in helping us to wage the war that is taking place in America today. I highly recommend *America at War* to all, especially those in full-time Christian service.

On September 11, 2001 our nation experienced a satanic attack – witnessed by the entire world. The terrorists that flew jetliners into American buildings represented an organization and religion that is anti-God and anti-American.

This same attack has been taking place, for many years, all over America. One of Satan's instruments of choice, for the destruction of this nation, has been our public school system, which the author again deals with in this book. His greatest advantage in using this weapon is that he is waging war against those who haven't the ability to counter attack. Much like September 11, the casualties are innocent and unprepared; they are the youth of our nation.

What can stop an attack of such magnitude? One way is knowledge. One September 11, a brave group of Americans stopped a fourth plane that was heading towards our capitol. The only reason something was done was because these men found out by cell phone about the other three planes at the World Trade Center and the Pentagon. It was only after they acquired this knowledge that something was done to protect the innocent lives in Washington D.C.

Read this book carefully. It in detail outlines the attack of Satan upon our country, and upon our children. The knowledge you gain from this book should cause you to stand and say, "Some way, some how, I must do something for those I know who are being attacked without warning."

Pastor, Gospel Light Baptist Church, Hot Springs, Arkansas

WORD ABOUT AMERICA

"Americans and Europeans sometimes forget how unique the United States of America is. No other nation has been created so swiftly and successfully. No other nation has been built upon an idea – the idea of liberty. No other nation has so successfully combined people of different races and nations within a single culture. Both the founding fathers of the United States and successive waves of immigrants to your country were determined to create a new identity.

Whether in flight from persecution or from poverty, the huddled masses have, with few exceptions, welcomed American values, the American way of life and American opportunities. And America herself has bound them to her with powerful bonds of patriotism and pride.

The European nations are not and can never be like this. They are the product of history and not a philosophy. You can construct a nation on an idea; but you cannot reconstruct a nation on the basis of one."

-The Retired Honorable Margaret Thatcher, 1991

PREFACE

America, the "land of the free and home of the brave." Oh, how times have changed. A nation that once was considered the greatest in the world (and she still is), the embodiment of all that was right and good, a light in the midst of a dark and dying world, and a bastion for the entire world to trust has changed dramatically over the past fifty years.

As Americans, we have been blessed because there came before us men and women who were willing to pay the price for their freedom, and the freedom of their children, but also for our freedom over 200 years later. Former president John Quincy Adams was right when he said, "Posterity – you will never know how much it has cost my generation to preserve your freedom. I hope you will make good use of it."

Unfortunately, here we are in the twenty-first century and we are not making "good use of it." Why is this so? Thomas Paine answered this question for us in 1776 saying, "What we obtain too cheaply, we esteem too lightly."

After receiving Canaan, the land of promise, Israel prospered beyond all the surrounding nations, and became the envy of all. Nevertheless, in due time, in spite of God's continual warnings, in the midst of her national prosperity and international popularity, Israel fell and she fell hard! She fell from her lofty position as a peculiar people, the chosen ones of God, and found herself in bondage to her Babylonian "neighbors."

The United States of America has followed in the footsteps of the Old Testament people of God traveling the paths of idolatry, immorality, and indecency. The secularist, humanist and atheist, though still in the minority, have taken control of the "high places" in our society and have been faithfully, fervently and feverishly fighting for the right to a "secular state," a nation that has forgotten and forsaken God. Our adversaries have always understood that before our nation could be conquered, "its faith must be uprooted."[1] Unfortunately, we haven't been faithfully fighting the "good fight of faith," and we have let this nation go to hell. Thus our adversaries and their dream of converting our nation into a "secular state" is becoming a reality right before our eyes.

Our sole purpose in writing this book is to reveal the truth, that **America is at war**; and that we are battling for the soul and the future of our nation. This book will not be politically correct; it may even be controversial, especially when we deal with the sins of abortion and homosexuality. I am convinced that these two abominations have brought the judgment of God upon our land, and if we do not as a nation "repent," we will regret!

Concerning controversy, Dr. Gresham Machan once said, "If you have the peace of God in your heart, you will never shrink from controversy; you will never be afraid to earnestly contend for the faith."

This book will bring to our remembrance how our forefathers lived, what they believed, what they envisioned, and how far we have come from their ideals. In addition, this book will help us to understand what we must know and do, if we are to ever reclaim this land for the glory of God and for the good of our children, and our children's children. *America at War: The Battle for the Future of Our Nation* is my attempt to say with former presidential candidate, Patrick Buchanan, "Traditionalists can run but they cannot hide."

It's high time we quit running and quit trying to hide. It's time to get in the battle for the soul of our country. As one author warned, "Never let up in this war between good and evil. It will be God's law or man's law."[2]

- INTRODUCTION -

The United States of America was and still is the greatest nation in the world. America is not only the greatest nation in the world, but also the greatest nation in the history of the world. Very few would attempt to refute this statement, unless they have been "brainwashed" by the liberal Marxist professors in our supposed schools of "higher learning."

What made this nation great? Was it our material resources and wealth? Was it our mighty spirit of individualism? What made America great? America's greatness found its source in the blessing and bounty of the God of Heaven. Few, if any nations, outside of Israel herself, could boast of the blessings of God more so than the United States of America. Author George Boddis has rightly said, "The providence of God is no more clearly seen in the history of any nation than in that of America. Indeed, if we read our national history in the light of the Scripture, we can see God's hand in American history as clearly as that in Israel."[3]

Unfortunately, so few of us recognize these blessings and benefits. Thomas Jefferson was correct in his declaration, "Its soul, its climate, its equality, liberty, laws, people, and manners- my God! How little do my countrymen know what precious blessings they are in possession of, and which no other people enjoy."

AMERICA – A CHRISTIAN HERITAGE

It is our heritage as a people, yes, our Christian heritage, which made this nation the greatest nation in the history of the world. In 1831, Alexis de Tocqueville, a French scholar and historian, came to America searching for her greatness. So impressed, with our "Christian" culture and our constitutional form of government, he published an exhaustive, two volume description of our nation that is still a classic today. Let's hear from *Democracy in America*:

> On my arrival in the United States *the religious aspect of the country* was the first thing that struck my attention; and the longer I stayed there, the more I perceived the great political consequences resulting from this new state of things. In France, I had almost always seen the spirit of religion and the spirit of freedom marching in opposite directions. *But in America I found they were intimately united and that they reigned in common over the same country.*[4]

He continued by saying,

> Religion ... must be regarded as the first of their political institutions ... I do not know whether all Americans have a sincere faith in their religion – for who can search the human heart? – But I am certain that they hold it to be indispensable to the maintenance of republican institutions. ... The sects (Christian denominations) that exist in the United States are innumerable. ... Moreover, all the sects of the United States are comprised within the great unity of Christianity, and Christian morality is everywhere the same.
>
> In the United States, the sovereign authority is religious ... there is no country in the world where the Christian religion retains a greater influence over the souls of men than in America ... *Christianity, therefore, reigns without obstacle.*[5]

18

This nation was founded upon biblical principles, and there are many who believe that this nation was founded to be a gospel "lighthouse" for the world. Since the arrival of our Pilgrim forefathers in 1620, and for the next 300 years or more, this nation was, without a doubt, a Christian nation. As the Puritan John Winthrop declared, this nation was founded as a "city set on a hill" to shed the light of God's Word amidst the darkness of the world. Dr. R. G. Lee, the great Baptist orator, once declared, "Who, knowing the facts of our history, can doubt that the United States of America has been a thought in the mind of God from all eternity?"

As a nation, we had a glorious and a godly beginning. As we shall see in chapter three, this nation was founded a Christian nation; this is a historical fact that cannot be denied. But something has gone wrong–terribly wrong! We have strayed far from our spiritual roots. We are definitely not the same nation that once was the envy of the world. Anyone over the age of fifty is tempted to look at our nation as a different country from the one they knew as a child.

WE'VE DRIFTED

It seems that helplessness and hopelessness are abounding in our once pious, proud and prosperous nation. Many of us find ourselves wondering how and why this nation has changed so dramatically and in such a short period of time. Our reflections seldom stop there – we also find ourselves contemplating just how much worse can things get? Also, we find ourselves asking, "is considerable improvement even a possibility?" It would appear that the "American Dream" is gradually becoming the "American Nightmare."

For much of our history, we really were "One Nation Under God," but that has changed. For nearly sixty to seventy years now, our nation has been "engulfed" in a great conflict, or as some have called it, a "Culture War." The conflict that currently engulfs America, as well as other Western nations, is designed to dethrone Jesus Christ from His rightful place as Lord of all, and replace our biblical worldview with a secular worldview. This attack on Christian ideals has come "from a variety of different directions and in a number of areas."[6] Concerning the impact and influence of this cultural conflict, former Judge Robert Bork, was accurate stating, "Not a single American institution, from popular music to higher education to science, has remained untouched."[7]

A DECLARATION OF WAR

On Wednesday, June 27, 2002 a federal appeals court in California triggered outrage across America (and well it should have) by foolishly and fiendishly declaring that the simple recitation of the Pledge of the Allegiance in "public schools" was unconstitutional. Why? Because the phrase "one nation under God," according to the liberal left, is a violation of the First Amendment of our U.S. Constitution. Of course, as we shall see in this book, this is a blatant lie of the devil and his demonic and despicable disciples that are working tirelessly at destroying the "values" and the "vision" of our nation.

There is, has been, and will continue to be a great cosmic struggle for the soul of this nation. Some have referred to this war as a "Great Civil War" that is being fought over contrasting and conflicting worldviews – a battle for the minds of our children and the soul of our country. As we shall see, this divide is one over the "values and vision" that will dominate our country, not only today, but also in years to come. No doubt, we are in the midst of a battle for the future of our nation.

I love America but I do not love what she has become. Something is wrong. It's high time for a change to take place in this country. Changes, real changes of substance, will not take place until we, the people of God, rise up and declare war on the "enemies of the cross."

America is at War; it's high time we as Christians make the declaration and get on with the business of the battle. Raging in our nation at this very moment is a war that will determine the fate of our nation in the far off future. Our Constitutional Republic founded over 225 years ago, without a doubt, is facing a time like no other in our nation's history. The only time period in our history that can even compare would be the great Civil War that divided our nation in two and almost destroyed the "great experiment" of our Founding Fathers.

Of course, the battle that is being waged in America today is not one of bullets and bombs, but one of "values" and "vision." The ideology of our Founding Fathers, and the principles laid out in the Holy Scripture, are being attacked by enemies of the cross today. Karl Marx, the founder of Communism, who believed that "Religion was the opiate of the masses," believed in the divinity of the "state" and that all religion should be eliminated. The spirit of Marx lives on in America today.

Regrettably, as the battle is raging, many of us don't even recognize that there is a battle. As one author has stated, "Unfortunately, so many people who share traditionalist views appear not to know a war is going on – a conflict that will have profound implications for future generations. By contrast, our opponents are highly motivated, well funded, deeply committed, and armed to the teeth. Secular humanists, particularly the more radical activists, have a specific agenda in mind for the future of our children, for our nation, and for our world."

TOO LITTLE TOO LATE

Chief Justice Earl Warren once said, "I like to believe we are living today in the spirit of the Christian religion. I also like to believe that as long as we do so, no great harm can come to our country."[8] Someone has rightly said, "America is running on the momentum of a godly heritage and when the momentum is spent, God help us!" Still another has reminded us, "History is filled with the wreckage of nations that have become indifferent to God, and died."[9] The late General Douglas MacArthur once noted:

> The history in war can be summed up in two words: *too late*. Too late in comprehending the deadly purpose of a potential enemy; too late in realizing the mortal danger; too late in preparedness; too late in uniting all possible forces for resistance; too late in standing with one's friends.[10]

Like Israel of old, God intended a divine purpose for this nation and intended for us to be a fruitful vineyard for the good of the world and the glory of God. Unfortunately, instead of bringing forth fruit that remains (John 15:1-8, 16), as a nation we have produced "wild grapes" (Isaiah 5:1-8). God's "universal" and unchanging principle of "sowing and reaping" (Galatians 6:7) has been set in motion as we have "sown to the flesh."

God has been removed from the halls of our government buildings, our nation's classrooms, and most of our churches. The Constitution, though paid lip service by those in authority, has been scrapped. And most people have been seduced into accepting the diabolically obscene humanist dogma that they evolved from slime. That the United States is headed for judgment day is beyond dispute. God is not mocked. What we have sown, that we will surely reap!

My prayer is that this book will be used in a small way to awaken the people of Zion to the fact that, "the momentum is spent," and if we don't do something – before it's too late, Biblical Christianity will become extinct.

- CHAPTER 1 -

FRIENDS, WE ARE AT WAR

"This charge I commit unto thee, son, Timothy ... that thou by them mightest war a good warfare."

- 1 Timothy 1:18

America is at war. The Bible, once our conscience and moral compass, has been eliminated from the public schools and the public square. We have sat back and allowed the "enemies of the cross," who hold nothing to be sacred or sure, to revise our history books and remove our heritage as a Christian nation founded upon Biblical principles. The Scripture says, *"Blessed is the nation whose God is the Lord"* (Psalm 33:12). America has forgotten its godly foundation on which she was built. We have exchanged the truth of God's Word for the lies of a godless world. We have traded our spiritual birthright as a God-fearing nation for the socialist, humanistic and atheistic pottage of the day. *We are battling for the future of our nation!*

AMERICA IS AT WAR. Though our money says, "In God we trust," we have become a nation that has placed her trust in government rather than God. We have exchanged moral living for materialistic living, and we have forsaken the God of our Fathers. We have apathetically sat back and watched over forty million children butchered, watched the education system perverted, the entertainment industry polluted, and have allowed the "Sodomites" to come out of the closet and take permanent residence as typical Americans. Like Sodom of old, we have pushed morals aside and become a nihilistic society that has

25

rejected truth and accepted moral relativism as the godless guiding principles of the day. *We are battling for the future of our nation!*

AMERICA IS AT WAR. Our government has not only legalized but is also actually funding the "butchering" of America children at a rate of approximately 5,000 per day. To make matters worse, our young people, your child and mine, can step into a government-run human butcher shop and have her child murdered without our knowledge, and we pay for it. Our government has also deemed it necessary to pass out condoms to our children, again without our knowledge, and again, we get to pay for it! Something is wrong with this picture. *We are battling for the future of our nation!*

AMERICA IS AT WAR. The U.S. Supreme Court in effect declares the reading of the Declaration of Independence at a high school graduation, as unconstitutional, due to its references to Almighty God. The **Ninth District Court of Appeals**, with jurisdiction over 20 percent of our nation, rules that it is unconstitutional to say the pledge of the allegiance, using the phrase "under God." Our Supreme Court Justices do not have enough sense to know that child pornography, whether real or computer simulated, is detrimental and destructive, and has resulted in a rash of sick and senseless killings. For the past half a century, our U.S. Supreme Court has declared war against God and all that is godly. *We are battling for the future of our nation!*

AMERICA IS AT WAR. Public school teachers may (and they do) describe the most hideous and hellish sexual acts in a classroom filled with impressionable minds – and it is legal! At the same time, and in the same classroom, it is illegal to hang a copy of the Ten Commandments, and to teach creation alongside of the theory of evolution. A ten-year-old child is "rebuked" by school officials for quietly reading her Bible on a school bus, but dozens of children and teens are using the most vulgar and graphic language on the same bus, as long as it is not loud enough to give the driver a headache. *We are battling for the future of our nation!*

AMERICA IS AT WAR. Television daily bombards the senses of our nation with the idea that wrong is right, that abnormal is normal, and the abhorrent is acceptable, and that what God calls an abomination is nothing more than an alternative life-style; it has its effect! Thirty years ago, the number one television show was the *Andy Griffith Show* – look how far we have come. *Jerry Springer* – need I say anymore? Hollywood celebrities openly and arrogantly flaunt their indecent and immoral relationships, including the vile practice of homosexuality. *We are battling for the future of our nation!*

AMERICA IS AT WAR. Sinister forces have tirelessly worked at redefining the family in America. Social organizations, like the Boy Scouts, have taken a stand against the perverts and because of it, are censured, and treated like second-class citizens. Politicians, yes even "conservative" politicians, are cow-towing to the homosexual lobby. Rock and rap music have deteriorated to a place where songs that call for the ambushing of police officers, murder of parents, sexually abusing women and suicide climb to the top of the charts faster than you can say, "The Beatles." *We are battling for the future of our nation!*

AMERICA IS AT WAR. Many of our churches, once great lighthouses where God's Word was thundered from pulpits "aflame with righteousness," have become nothing more than secular social centers where everyone but God "feels good."

While our enemies work tirelessly to advance their cause, we have very few men who will stand up for what is right regardless of the consequences, and who will champion the great causes of the Bible. *We are battling for the future of our nation!*

AMERICA IS AT WAR. Unfortunately, many of God's people are AWOL. God give us men who are *"strong in the grace that is in Christ Jesus"* (2 Tim 2:1), and who are willing to *"endure hardness, as a good soldier of Jesus Christ"* (2 Tim 2:3). May the God of Heaven raise up men who are willing to go to war, and not *"entangleth himself with the affairs of this life"* (2 Tim 2:4a). Of course, the purpose is to *"please Him [Jesus] who hath chosen him to be a soldier"* (2 Tim 2:4b). *We are battling for the future of our nation!*

AMERICA IS AT WAR. The people of God had better wake up and realize these are not days of peace and prosperity; these are days of war. Let us not be guilty of saying, *"Peace, peace; when there is no peace"* (Jeremiah 6:14). The battle isn't ours, it is the Lord's, but the Lord is calling for soldiers who are willing to *"Fight the good fight of faith"* (1 Timothy 6:12), and who recognize that there is no middle ground in this fight. We are either fighting for the Lord or we are *"found even to fight against the Lord"* (Acts 5:39). It is good to know that *"The Lord shall fight for [us]"* (Exodus 14:14), and that *"the battle is the Lord's"* (1 Samuel 17:47), but we must all do our part. *We are battling for the future of our nation!*

FOLKS, AMERICA IS AT WAR! The battle is for the future of our nation. Someone will win this battle, someone will take this land, someone will eventually control the high ground in our society – who will it be? Just as England's Parliament and King George III placed our Founders "between a rock and a hard place," we today are being forced into a corner by the secular humanists that would destroy everything this nation was founded upon. For the sake of our children and our country, may God grant us the grace to not only get in the battle, but also fight to win. In his famous words supporting our War for Independence, Patrick Henry said in 1775:

> ... [W] e must fight! I repeat it, sir, we must fight! An appeal to arms and to the God of hosts is all that is left us! Besides, sir, we shall not fight our battles alone. There is a just God who presides over the destinies of nations, and Who will raise up friends to fight our battles for us. The battle, sir, is not to the strong alone; it is to the vigilant, the active, the brave. ... Our chains are forged! Their clanking can be heard on the plains of Boston! The war is inevitable—and let it come! I repeat it, sir, let it come.

> ... Gentlemen may cry, Peace, Peace—but there is no peace. The war is actually begun! The next gale that sweeps from the north will bring to our ears the clash of resounding arms! Our brethren are already in the field! Why stand we here idle? What is it that gentlemen wish? What would they have? Is life so dear, or peace so sweet, as to be purchased at the price of chains and slavery? Forbid it, Almighty God! I know not what course others may take; but as for me, give me liberty or give me death! [11]

We want America back, back to what she was founded to be by our Founding Fathers, back to what God originally intended for this nation. God give us some men with the "spirit of Patrick Henry" – Men who are willing to live and die for a cause!

We need a great army of committed soldiers of the cross to "rise up and be doing" the work of the kingdom. We need men, women and young people who will take the Great Commission seriously, and who will voice their opinions and do what they can to stem the tide of secular humanism, atheism and paganism in our nation. We must not only hold our ground, but we must also be willing to "take the land" back from the demonic and deceptive activists who have literally transformed this nation into a secular state that has forsaken God.

Politicians and programs will not, and cannot, save this nation. However, God can and will, if we will fulfill the scriptural mandate as found in **II Chronicles 7:14-15**. Christian revival must precede cultural renewal. Folks, no revival – no renewal! The words of Phillip M. Crane, for many years a Republican Representative from Illinois, are extremely enlightening. Crane wrote:

> *FRIENDS, WE ARE AT WAR!* We are battling for the soul of this Republic. Scriptural authority is in retreat. Instead of fearing God, we fear government. Instead of looking to God to guide us, we look to government to solve our problems. Instead of guarding our liberties, we seem eager to barter them for security ...

> **Why is this so?** Solzhenitsyn said it this way: "When one sees your free and independent life, all the dangers I talk about seem imaginary ... But this carefree life cannot continue ... A concentration of world evil, of hatred for humanity, is taking place, and is fully determined to destroy our society."

> More than two hundred years ago, a man named Thomas Paine wrote a pamphlet called *Common Sense*. With clear and precise logic, he helped them to understand the nature of the enemy; he prodded them to commit their lives, their fortunes and their sacred honor, to the most significant battle the world has ever known.

> Long before Thomas Paine, the Lord God made it clear, in His Word, "Righteousness exalteth a nation, but sin is a reproach to any people." The Bible tells us, and history attests, that "When the righteous are in authority the people rejoice; but when the wicked bears rule, the people mourn." These words, like all scriptural solutions to man's dilemma represent eternal, *uncommon sense*. An uncommon sense sorely needed for times as these that "truly try men's souls."

The phrase "the battle is the Lord's" was echoed by a young shepherd boy David, in the face of a great calamity for the people of God, while the mighty warriors of Israel *"fled from him (Goliath), and were sore afraid"* (1 Samuel 17:24). David courageously stood his ground while his brothers cowered. David was willing to fight while his brother chose to flee. David, on his own, enlisted as a soldier in the Lord's army while his military brethren refused to "fight the good fight." God give us some more young men like David!

Ephesians 6:10-13, Finally, my brethren, be strong in the Lord, and in the power of His might. Put on the whole armour of God, that ye may be able to stand against the wiles of the devil. For we wrestle not against flesh and blood, but against principalities, against powers, against the rulers of the darkness of this world, against spiritual wickedness in high places. Wherefore take unto you the whole armour of God that ye may be able to withstand in the evil day, and having done all, to stand.

The Scriptures make it clear, **WE ARE AT WAR**. Our battle is spiritual, but we are to engage in the battle in the physical realm. If we are not willing to fight, we lose the war by default and literally hand our country over to the enemy. Daniel Webster clearly stated, "God grants liberty only to those who love it, and are always ready to guard and defend it."[12] May God grant the grace to see, in America, a mighty army of patriots who are consecrated unto God and consumed with a cause that is greater than they are. The words of David still ring true today, **"Is there not a cause?"** Of course, the answer is a resounding yes.

AMERICA IS AT WAR – WE ARE BATTLING FOR THE FUTURE OF OUR NATION!

- CHAPTER 2 -

THE IMPORTANCE
OF HISTORY

*"That this may be a sign among you, that when your
children ask their fathers in time to come, saying, What
mean ye by these stones? Then ye shall answer them, That
the waters of Jordan were cut off before the ark of the
covenant of the LORD; when it passed over Jordan, the
waters of Jordan were cut off: and these stones shall be for
a memorial unto the children of Israel for ever."*

- Joshua 4:6-7

We live in a day and age in which good old American history doesn't seem to count for much anymore. Truth is, most government-run schools no longer teach "real" American history. If they teach it at all, it is a watered-down politically correct all-you-can-eat selection of multi-cultural hogwash. Could this be one reason that a great majority of young men in college have repeatedly stated they would not be willing to go to war to defend America?

To obtain volunteers for the war, we must first be able to convince men, women and young people that there is something worth fighting for, something worth laying down our comforts and conveniences for, something that we can call a worthwhile "cause." Alas, this is not always an easy job.

33

Concerning what our adversaries have done to America, one author has concluded that they "have replaced the good country we grew up in with a cultural wasteland and a moral sewer that are not worth living in and not worth fighting for – their country, not ours."[13] The renowned, Edmund Burke once said, "To make us love our country, our country ought to be lovely."[14] In far too many ways, as Pat Buchanan said:

> America is no longer lovely. Though she remains a great country, many wonder if she is still a good country. [O] ur world has been turned upside down. What was right and true yesterday is wrong and false today. What was immoral and shameful–promiscuity, abortion, euthanasia, suicide–has become praiseworthy. Nietzsche called it the transvaluation of all values; the old virtues become sins, and the old sins become virtues.[15]

For certain, one of the reasons America has lost her "beauty" is because she has lost her sense of destiny. American Christians on the whole have lost their sense of destiny because they haven't the knowledge that God predestined this nation for His purposes. Former president Woodrow Wilson reminds us, "A nation which does not remember what it was yesterday, does not know what it is today, nor what it is trying to do. We are trying to do a futile thing if we do not know where we came from or what we have been about."

Winston Churchill was correct in his observation. "The greatest advances in human civilization have come when we recovered what we had lost." It is important that we look back in our past so that we might understand the truth about how and why our nation was formed. May God help us to recover what we have lost! It was this same Churchill who said, "The farther backward you can look, the farther forward you are likely to see."

I am not sure if truer and more relevant words have ever been spoken than those of Pulitzer Prize-winning historian Daniel J. Boorstin, who once said, "Americans are so ignorant of their past that they have become 'prisoners' of the present ... Obsessed with where we are, have we forgotten where we came from and how we got here."[16]

What we believe about the past greatly determines how we live in the present, and ultimately results in either the blessing or the curse of God upon this land. Therefore, it would be to our benefit to know the truth that can set us free from these present days of ignorance, idolatry and immorality. Vile myths are permeating our society and have transformed our belief system, not only as individuals, but also as a nation.

Understanding the vision and values of our past will enable us to have a clearer and more viable vision for our future. Patrick Henry stated it well, when he said: "I have no light to illuminate the pathway of the future save that which falls over my shoulder from the past." Another reminds us, "We live in the present, we dream of the future, but we learn eternal truths from the past." And yet still another said, "If men could learn from history, what lessons it might teach us!"

One of the most tenacious and tragic myths of our times is that the founding fathers were dedicated to the secularization of our society. There are many – some sinister, some sincere, who would have us believe that the Founding of the United States was "a dedicated exercise in secularization by Deists, rationalists, and freethinkers," a collection of men "who wanted to subvert any form of Christian political order, breaking decisively with the inherited Christian civilization of Europe."[17]

As author George Grant wrote, "Not only is it perilously imprudent to ignore history, but it is equally imprudent to ignore the hand of God in shaping it." Grant also reminds us that even "a wrinkle in time bears the obvious impress of God's own good providence.[18]

Sadly, not only are we ignoring history, but also God has been kicked off our school campuses and He has been deleted from our history books by God-hating history revisionists. Again, Grant sets the record straight declaring: "Modern historians can agree on very few things. But when it comes to God, there is a sudden consensus. The long-held notion that history is His story is fiercely resisted in our day."[19] Over the past sixty to seventy years our adversaries, the "enemies of the cross" have done everything within their power to bring a new understanding of the historical records.

Alexander Solzhenitzyn once declared, "To destroy a people, you must sever their roots." Not surprisingly, the way one can sever a people's roots is by destroying its memory. If you can deprive a people the true knowledge of who they are and where they came from you can begin to lay the foundation for a new society. In the words of former president Ronald Reagan:

> If we forget what we did, we won't know who we are. I am warning of the eradication of … the American memory, [which] could result, ultimately, in an erosion of the American spirit.[20]

For a modern state the formula for erasing memory was given to us by Fabian Socialist H.G. Orwell who said, "Who controls the past controls the future. Who controls the present controls the past."[21] As Buchanan noted, "Destroy the record of a people's past, leave it in ignorance of who its ancestors were and what they did, and one can fill the empty vessels of their souls with a new history … Dishonor or disgrace a nation's heroes, and you can demoralize its people."[22]

CHANGING THE HISTORY BOOKS

"He who controls the past controls the future. He who controls the present controls the past."

Dr. Paul C. Vitz, New York University psychology professor, did a research project for the U.S. Department of Education on sixty of the most accepted textbooks in our public schools. It is projected that 87 percent of the nation's school children use these books. "The most striking thing about these texts," stated Dr. Vitz in Judge Brevard Hand's court in Mobile, Alabama, "is the total absence of the Christian religion in them." Vitz went on to point out that "other beliefs were mentioned-the Jewish, Amish, Mormon, and Catholic faiths-but little or no mention was made of the evangelical Protestants who founded this nation."

Secularism is taught in those same textbooks, a life and worldview for children and young people that little resembles the one taught for the first 150 years in this nation's history. Very little mention is made of the public schools that represented education at the time of our Founding Fathers. Therefore, an entire generation of young people has been robbed of our wonderful Christian heritage and because of this, their worldview is far different from those of just a few decades ago.

SNEAKING IN SOCIALISM

America's transition from a sovereign constitutional republic to a socialist democracy would come through the government-run school system. "Socialism" – could this be what "Frontier

Thinker" and progressive "educrat" Harold Rugg had in mind when he wrote in *The Great Technology*:

> A new public mind is to be created. How? Only by creating tens of millions of individual minds and welding them into a new social mind. Old stereotypes must be broken up and new climates of opinion formed in the neighborhoods of America...*through the schools of the world, we shall disseminate a new conception of government – one that will embrace all the activities of men...*[23]

As far as Harold Rugg was concerned, every problem in society could eventually be solved by allowing, "the social engineers [to] take care of the details."[24] Rugg was committed to make education work by giving "it a driving purpose, so clear and magnetic that thousands of teachers and millions of parents and youth will be energized by it."[25] As one author declared, "Today, millions of Americans who were educated on Rugg's readable and crusading textbooks are ruled by his ideas – and by his chaos."

Five million children "learned" American political and economic history in the progressive era, especially the 1930's from fourteen social studies textbooks that Harold Rugg authored.[26] The Senate Investigating Committee on Education of the California legislature condemned the NEA-sponsored series for *subtly playing up Marxism and destroying American traditions.*[27] This same Rugg also produced the corresponding teacher's guides, course outlines, and student workbooks.

So blatant was the downgrading of American heroes and the U.S. Constitution, so pronounced was the anti-religious bias, so open was the propaganda for socialistic control that the public rebelled.[28] A Senate Committee report "found among other things that 113 Communist-front organizations had to do with some of the material in the books and that 50 Communist front authors were connected with it."[29]

REECE COMMITTEE

Norman Dodd, director of research for the Reece Committee, established by the U.S. Congress in 1954, revealed that a study of the activities of tax-free foundations in this country during the past fifty years indicated that some of their enormous resources had been used ($30 million a year from *Carnegie* alone, plus the *Rockefeller* and *Ford Foundations*) to change the perception of history. Instead of presenting our national heroes like George Washington, Thomas Jefferson, Benjamin Franklin, and others as men of virtue, they were purposely presented as crass human beings who used their public notoriety for personal advantage. As one author declared:

> This gave substance to the report of the 1950's that textbooks were purposely changed to include moral indiscretions, suggesting even that Thomas Jefferson had fathered children by one of his slave girls-a report that rests on very dubious "evidence." This reduction of national heroes was what caused some of the angry parental outcries of the '60s and '70s to the effect that textbooks gave more space to Marilyn Monroe than to our Founding Fathers.

> Thus, a whole generation of young people grew up without the knowledge of American heroes, which contributed to a loss of patriotism and the reluctance of young men to serve in our military service.[30]

Norman Dodd, in a video testimony to a Dallas doctor, explained how the *Carnegie Foundation* board had designed the rewriting of history. In the beginning they tried to hire scholars to create new books that emphasized the fallacies about our nation's heroes. To the tribute of the scholars in 1904-1910, the

Carnegie board couldn't find any who would agree to do it. But the board did find sharp young collegians, sent them to graduate school, and then financed them to "rewrite" history to conform to what is today called "a contemporary view of history." Roy R. Friday has written a pamphlet entitled *My Weekly Brainwash.* Note a portion of the opening paragraph:

> For the past two decades I have been watching this insidious propaganda take its toll. In the schools ... the seedlings of socialism are eating away the foundations of our Constitutional Republic like termites. *They are selling our heritage, our children, and our future as a great republic right down the river.*[31]

What is being taught in the textbooks of our nation's government-run schools is literally transforming and turning this generation away from God. Young people of every age have derived their values, not only from their parents, but also from their teachers and their textbooks. One humanist author makes this clear when he says, "Let me publish the textbooks of nations, and I care not who writes its songs or makes its laws."[32]

AMERICA'S HEALTH IS DEPENDENT UPON UNDERSTANDING HER HERITAGE

"A historical awareness is essential for the health and well-being of any society; it enables us to know who we are, why we are here, and what we should do. Just as a loss of memory in an individual is a psychiatric defect calling for medical treatment, so too any community which has no social memory is suffering from an illness."[33] *- Historian, John Briggs*

English author and lecturer John H.Y. Briggs has movingly declared that it is vital for the health of a nation to know and understand its roots – its spiritual heritage, if you will. Many of the spiritual sicknesses that have plagued our nation are the result of misunderstanding or neglecting our spiritual heritage as a Christian nation. As one author has written, "No other national story holds such tremendous lessons, for the American people themselves and for the rest of mankind."[34]

In the words of Thomas Jefferson, "History by apprising people of the past will enable them to judge ... the future." Jefferson was right; we cannot rightly judge the present, let alone the future, if we do not have a clear understanding of our past. Our history as a nation now spans four centuries and, as we have now just entered into a new millennium, we must retell it, for if we can discover the truth about America, and build upon that truth we, along with our "generations to come," will benefit from it.

"My extensive readings have left me without a doubt that this nation was founded by Christians and was meant to be based on broad Christian principles. Religion was the bedrock upon which the nation stood, and without it these amazing men and women saw no future for the country they had established."[35]

– RABBI DANIEL LAPIN

- CHAPTER 3 -

OUR CHRISTIAN HERITAGE

"Blessed is the nation whose God is the Lord; and the people whom He hath chosen for His own inheritance."

- Psalm 33:12

Nations are classified in different ways. Case in point, by their form of government. One is a kingdom, another is an empire, and yet, still another a republic. We not only classify nations by form of government, but we classify nations by race also. Great Britain is an Anglo-Saxon nation, France a Gallic, Germany a Teutonic, Russia a Slav. Nations are often classified by religion or their religious heritage. One is a Mohammedan nation, others are heathen nations, and still others are Christian nations.[36] The United States of America is, and always has been, classified among the Christian nations of the world. As Associate Supreme Court Justice David Brewer wrote:

> But in what sense can it be called a Christian nation? Not in the sense that Christianity is the established religion or that the people are in any manner compelled to support it. On the contrary, the constitution specifically provides that "Congress shall make no law respecting an establishment of religion, or prohibiting the free exercise thereof." Neither is it Christian in the sense that all its citizens are either in fact or name Christians. ... Nevertheless, we constantly speak of this republic as a Christian nation – in fact, as the leading Christian nation in the world.[37]

The establishment of the United States of America is the "greatest of all human adventures." In 1905 former Associate Supreme Court Justice David Brewer noted, "Christianity was a

43

principal cause of the settlements on these western shores. It has been identified with the growth and development of those settlements into the United States of America, and has so largely shaped and molded it that today of all the nations in the world it is the most justly called *a Christian nation*."[38]

Justice Brewer continues, "I insist that Christianity has been so wrought into the history of this republic, so identified with its growth and prosperity, has been and is so dear to the hearts of the great body of our citizens, that it ought not to be spoken of contemptuously or treated with ridicule."[39] He also declared, we "who are citizens of this republic – recognizing the identification of Christianity with its life, the general belief that Christianity is the best of all religions…"[40]

SEEKING GOD NOT GOLD

"South America was settled by the Spanish, who came to South America in search of gold; North America was settled by the Pilgrim Fathers, who went there in search of God." - President of Argentina

A casual look at our history, before the many recent revisions, of course, enables us to come to the simple conclusion that our nation was founded upon a faith in the Word of God and a desire to do the will of God. Roger Babson, the statistician, was lunching with the President of Argentina when he was asked, "Mr. Babson, I have been wondering why it is that South America with all of its natural advantages, its mines of iron, copper, coal, silver and gold; its rivers and great waterfalls which rival Niagara, is so far behind North America." Babson replied: "Well Mr. President, what do you think is the reason?" Argentina's president was silent for a while before answering:

> I have come to this conclusion, South America was settled by the Spanish, who came to South America in search of gold; but North America was settled by the Pilgrim Fathers, who went there in search of God.[41]

The president's conclusion, the difference between the English settlers and the Spanish Conquistadors, was what they were seeking. The English came seeking God, while the Spanish came seeking gold.

God has abundantly blessed our nation because many of our forefathers sought the person and purpose of Christ, and were submitted to the principles of Christ. Listen to the words of our former President, Ronald Reagan at a prayer breakfast in 1982:

> I've always believed that we were, each of us, put here for a reason. That there is a plan, somehow a divine plan for all of us. I know now that whatever days are left of me belong to Him. I also believe this blessed land was set apart in a very special way. A country created by men and women who came here not in search of gold, but in search of God. They would be a free people, living under the law with faith in their maker and their future.

> Sometimes, it seems we've strayed from that noble beginning, from our conviction that standards of right and wrong do exist and must be lived up to. God, the source of our knowledge has been expelled from the classroom. He gives us His greatest blessing: life–and yet many would condone the taking of innocent life. We expect Him to protect us in a crisis, but turn away from Him too often in our day-to-day living. And I wonder if He isn't waiting for us to wake up.[42]

THE EARLY COLONIES

Contrary to what we have often been led to believe, "early America was a Christian society." From the founding of the colonies through the years of the Civil War and beyond, "Christianity was virtually the only religion professed by Americans."[43] In the first hundred years or so of our nation's history, individual believers and the church of Jesus Christ, prospered with liberation never experienced before in the history of the world, so much so that both de Tocqueville and Philip Schaff noted the great strength of Christianity in America. Schaff proclaimed, "The United States is by far the most religious and Christian country in the world ..."

A good majority of the early settlers looked upon America as a "promised land," and they sincerely "believed that they would be held accountable by Almighty God for the manner in which they developed and governed their new home."[44] The old puritan, John Winthrop declared:

> We shall be as a city set on a hill. The eyes of all people are upon us, so if we shall deal falsely with our God in this work we have undertaken and so cause Him to withdraw His present help from us, we shall be made a story and a by-word throughout the world.

As the puritan Winthrop declared, this nation was founded as a "city set on a hill" to shed the light of God's Word amidst the darkness of the world. America has been labeled "a Christian nation," not because it was founded as such, but because our Founding Fathers were Christians or had been influenced throughout their entire lives by the Christian consensus that surrounded them.

Historian and author, Archie Jones, affirms what dozens of others have verified, "Early American culture and thought had deep roots in the medieval period and were not merely Protestant but largely Calvinistic."[45] Author Loraine Boettner, wrote, "The importance of Calvinism to early American civilization and culture cannot be rightly doubted. Not only Christian but also non-Christian, not only Protestant but also Roman Catholic historians have affirmed this."[46] As Jones asserts, "Calvinism was certainly a great force for morality [and] a great political force, a force for justice and liberty."[47] Boettner also estimated that about two-thirds of early Americans at the time of our American Revolution were " trained in the school of Calvin."[48]

One author wrote that the American colonies had become "the most thoroughly Reformed, and Puritan commonwealths in the world," and declared that "Puritanism provided the moral and religious background of fully 75 percent of the people who declared their independence in 1776," and noted that if one were to include all the people "whose forbearers bore the 'stamp of Geneva' in some broader sense, 85 or 90 percent would not be an extravagant estimate."[49]

Early America was founded on the Scriptural principles of hard work, personal integrity, a closely-knit family unit, and a firm faith in the sovereignty of God. In addition, the strength of colonial America was not based on military power; it was based solely on *the character and moral fiber of the people*. Integrity, diligence, and productivity were taught and practiced as a way of life in colonial America. Strong and dynamic leaders were fashioned from this mold for many years. Our founders understood that "character counts." It has been said: "While the people are virtuous they cannot be subdued, but once they lose their virtue they will be ready to surrender their liberties to the first external or internal invader."[50]

During the time period, in which our nation was founded, two dominant philosophies or world views prevailed; one was spiritual, the other secular. For sure, there were many different variations of each of these views. Those who held to the secular worldview, including atheists and other skeptics, based their philosophy for living on a faulty foundation without God. This group was at best, a very small minority of the populace.

It is important that we understand that those with the spiritual or religious point of view had, as the foundation of their philosophical understanding, a belief in God as the Creator and Sustainer of the universe, including the world in which they lived. They also believed that man was responsible to obey God and His word, and accountable to God for the life in which he lived. Because of the great "Christian Consensus," and the spirit of a hard working people, God blessed this land in a way no other nation in the world had ever been blessed.

Psalms 85:1, "Lord, thou hast been favourable unto thy land."

NOT RELIGIOUS – A CHRISTIAN NATION

"It cannot be emphasized too strongly or too often that this great nation was founded, not by religionists, but by Christians, not on religions but on the gospel of Jesus Christ!" – Patrick Henry

It is apparent to all who are sincere and those who are willing to accept the truth concerning our past, that our forefathers, for the most part, were either Bible believing Christians, believed in God or had a basic respect for the Christian faith and our biblical values. They founded this country over two hundred years ago as One Nation Under God, and not just any God, but the God of the Bible. Furthermore, as we have already mentioned, it is also apparent that the providential hand of God has been behind America's blessing like no other nation in the world. Austin Sorenson wrote a great book *Is America Committing Suicide.* In it he stated:

> The blessings of a nation are dependent upon the favor of a sovereign God. Historically, our leaders have sought the guidance of the Almighty. America was born in greatness. The smile of Deity was upon us. The hand of God is seen in American history.[51]

There can be little doubt that America was founded on the principles found in the Holy Scriptures. Dr. Francis Schaeffer was right in referring to the theological, moral, and philosophical thought of early America as "the Christian consensus." Not all, but most of the colonists were Englishmen, and almost all were Europeans, who brought to the New World a Reformation mindset. Therefore, our government was based on a respect and reverence for the God of the Scriptures.

While our enemies are doing everything in their power to degrade, distort and deny the richness of our heritage, we have to candidly agree with Gary DeMar, who is much closer to the truth when he says:

> A study of America's past will show that a majority of Americans shared a common faith and a common ethic. America's earliest Founders were self-professing Christians and their founding documents expressed a belief in a Christian worldview.

Rabbi Daniel Lapin certainly has it right when he says:

> My extensive readings have left me without a doubt that this nation was founded by Christians, and was meant to be based on broad Christian principles. Religion was the bedrock upon which the nation stood, and without it these amazing men and women saw no future for the country they had established.[52]

49

Elsewhere in the same book Lapin says, "Christianity has been responsible among other things, for the founding of America, the greatest civilization the world has ever known, and for making America great."[53]

THE GREAT AWAKENING

The first Great Awakening had a great influence upon the men who would become our founding fathers, and the movement that would lead to the War for Independence. John Wingate Thornton was right when he said, "To the pulpit, the Puritan Pulpit, we owe the moral force which won our independence."[54]

As a result of the Great Awakening there was a great religious climate in the eighteenth century. "So religious was the climate … that even Benjamin Franklin, one of the founding fathers whom the humanists love to claim as their own, indicated that atheism was little known in the colonies."[55] Notice what Franklin wrote in a pamphlet entitled *Information to Those Who Would Remove to America*:

> Hence bad examples to youth are more rare in America, which must be a comfortable consideration to parents. To this may be truly added, that serious religion, under its various denominations, is not only tolerated, but respected and practiced. Atheism is unknown there; Infidelity rare and secret; so that persons may live to a great age in that country without having their piety shocked by meeting with either an Atheist or an Infidel.
>
> And the Divine Being seems to have manifested his approbation of the mutual forbearance and kindness with which the different sects treat each other, by the remarkable prosperity with which he has been pleased to favor the whole country.[56]

Benjamin Franklin also reported the results of the Great Awakening this way:

> It was wonderful to see the change soon made in the manners of our inhabitants. From being thoughtless or indifferent about religion, it seemed as if all the world were growing religious, so that one could not walk thro' the town in an evening without hearing psalms sung in different families of every street.[57]

As author John Stormer writes, "This was the atmosphere in which America was born. The people – and their schools and churches and government – were changed."[58] When George Whitfield preached in Boston, 22 preachers were converted. Even Harvard University, which later would become a battleground between Christianity and Unitarianism, was affected. Again, Stormer notes, "Some of our founding fathers were among the Harvard students who heard Whitfield preach in 1739. Others attended churches whose pulpits were filled by men converted under Whitfield's ministry – pulpits which were 'aflame with righteousness.'"[59]

America was born in this period of spiritual revival. It has been living since on the spiritual and political foundations laid by men who believed and obeyed God's command to "take the land."

UNIVERSALLY ACKNOWLEDGED

For the honest and sincere seeker of truth, history is clear, our founding father's embraced Christianity as the unofficial yet universally acknowledged religion of the land. From Benjamin Franklin's appeal for prayer at the Constitutional Convention of 1787, George Washington's Inaugural speech, to Abraham Lincoln's proclamation for "a day of national humiliation, fasting and prayer," we find a rich Christian heritage in American history. Associate Supreme Court Justice Joseph Story (1779-1845) makes this very clear stating:

> The real object of the First Amendment was not to countenance, much less to advance, Mohammedanism, or Judaism, or infidelity, by prostrating Christianity; but to exclude all rivalry among Christian sects, and to prevent any national ecclesiastical establishment which should give hierarchy the exclusive patronage of the national government.
>
> It thus cut off the means of religious persecution (the vice and pest of former ages) ... Probably at the time of the adoption of the constitution, and of the first amendment to it ... the general, if not universal, sentiment in America was that Christianity ought to receive encouragement from the State ...[60]

Christians have been criticized for referring to this country as a Christian nation. While the United States of America wasn't technically established for the advancement of the kingdom of God, many of the original colonies were. The more than four million citizens who shared in the founding of this republic were not only Christian, but also overwhelmingly Protestant. Even the state of Maryland, which was founded in part as a refuge for persecuted Catholics, welcomed very few Catholic immigrants prior to the Revolutionary War.

Mississippi Governor Kirk Fordice, with his infamous and insightful statement, "America is a Christian nation," stirred opposition from many fronts. Almost before finishing his statement, "he was being denounced as an intolerant bigot."[61] But why should folks become upset? The historical facts bear his statement to be true. Author and historian Gary DeMar, reminds us of a few of the facts:

> The earliest settlements in America were Protestant enterprises. Jews and Catholics were only tiny minorities.... In the First

Charter of Virginia, the colonists' declared goal is to "spread the Christian religion to such people as yet live in darkness and miserable ignorance of the true knowledge and worship of God."

"In the name of God, Amen" are the first six words of the Mayflower Compact, which proceeds, "by the grace of God.... having undertaken for the glory of God and advancement of the Christian faith...."

In the Fundamental Orders of Connecticut in 1639, the assembled declared, "The word of God requires that to maintain the peace and union of such a people there should be orderly and decent government established according to God...to preserve the liberty and purity of the Gospel of our Lord Jesus Christ."[62]

DeMar continues with a few more facts:

In 1892 the U.S. Supreme Court declared, "This is a Christian nation."[63] In this same decision we are reminded, "Our law and our institutions must necessarily be based upon and embody the teachings of the Redeemer of mankind. Our civilization and our institutions are emphatically Christian."

The then New Jersey Governor, later to become president of the United States, Woodrow Wilson unashamedly declared, "America was born a Christian nation – born to exemplify that devotion to the elements of righteousness which are derived from the revelations of the Holy Scripture."[64]

It wasn't only our early American heroes who recognized that our nation's glory and greatness came from God. Our 28th president, Woodrow Wilson recognized and reaffirmed America's greatness was due in large to her divine beginnings. He said, "...I believe that the glory of America is that she is a great spiritual conception and that in the spirit of her institutions dwells not only her distinction but her power...."[65] In 1905 Associate Supreme Court Justice Brewer rightly wrote:

It has been often said that Christian nations are the civilized nations, and as often that most thoroughly Christian are the most highly civilized. Is this a mere coincidence? Study well the history of Christianity in its relation to the nation and it will be found that it is something more than a mere coincidence, that there is between the two the relation of cause and effect, and that the more thoroughly the principles of Christianity reach into and influence the life of the nation the more certainly will that nation advance in civilization.[66]

The governor's "controversial" remarks landed him on CNN. His comments are perceptive and irrefutable. He said:

Christianity is the predominant religion in America. We all know that's an incontrovertible fact. The media always refer to the Jewish state of Israel. They talk about the Muslim country of Saudi Arabia, of Iran or Iraq. We all talk about the Hindu nation of India. America is not a "nothing" country. It's a Christian country.[67]

In 1931, Justice George Sutherland reaffirmed the court's 1892 decision, calling Americans "a Christian people."[68] Even Franklin D. Roosevelt, when crafting the Atlantic Charter with Winston Churchill, admitted that America was "founded on the principles of Christianity" and went on to lead the American and British sailors in "Onward Christian Soldier."[69] Harry Truman, in a letter to Pius XII, also affirmed, "This is a Christian nation."[70]

In a 1951 Supreme Court decision, Justice William Douglas wrote, "We are a religious people and our institutions presuppose the existence of a Supreme Being."[71] Listen to the words of our 34th president, Dwight D. Eisenhower who said, to a group in Israel, "… the peoples of Israel, like those of the United States, are imbued with a religious faith and a sense of moral values."

Former President Carter, admitted, "We have a responsibility to try to shape government so that it does exemplify the will of God."[72]   The earnest and honest student of American history cannot refute the fact that our nation was founded with a "Christian consensus" and based upon biblical principles. Justice J. Brewer in an address delivered at Harvard in 1905 made this clear. Brewer referred to Supreme Court cases, both at the state and federal level, along with numerous documents and state constitutions. Concluding his address, he boldly declared:

> In no charter or constitution is there anything to even suggest that any other than the Christian is the religion of this country ... In short, there is no charter or constitution that is either infidel, agnostic or non-Christian.[73]

In spite of what present day secular and sinister historians would have us to believe, "The prosperity and well-being of the United States wasn't an accident. It was mainly a matter of cause and effect; the effect was caused by a reverence for and a response to the laws and principles clearly laid out in God's Word."[74]

OUR FOUNDERS AND THE "SPIRIT OF 76"

Samuel Adams, one of the original "Sons of Liberty," understood clearly that our nation's independence from the tyranny of Britain was the result of God's purpose and plan. Listen to his words as he makes clear the reason for America's staggering successes against Britain. Adams said:

> We are now on this continent ... three millions of souls united in one common cause ... There are instances of, I would say, an almost astonishing Providence in our favor; our success has staggered our enemies, and almost given faith to infidels; so that

we might truly say it is not our own arm which has saved us. The hand of heaven appears to have led us on to be, perhaps, humble instruments and means in great providential dispensation, which is completing.[75]

Adams also gives credit where credit is due when he reminds us that God deserved to be praised for this great victory. He said "If it was ever granted mortals to trace the designs of Providence, and interpret its manifestations in favor of their cause, we may, with humility of soul, cry out, Not unto us, but to thy name be praise..." This same patriot also wrote in his pamphlet *The Rights of Colonists*:

The rights of colonists as Christians may best be understood by reading and carefully studying the institutes of the great lawgiver and the Head of the Christian church, which can be found in the New Testament.[76]

Concerning our victory in the War for Independence John Adams said:

The general principles on which the fathers achieved independence were ... the general principles of Christianity ... I will avow that I then believed, and now believe, that those general principles of Christianity are as eternal and immutable as the existence and attributes of God.[77]

In a speech given on July 4, 1837 John Quincy Adams (our sixth president) declared:

Why is that next to the birthday of the Savior of the world, your most joyous and most venerated festival returns on this day? Is it not that, in the chain of human events, the birthday of the nation is indissolubly linked with the birthday of the Savior. That it forms a leading event in the progress of the gospel dispensation?

Is it not that the Declaration of Independence first organized the social compact on the foundation of the Redeemer's mission upon earth? That it *laid the cornerstone of human government upon the first precepts of Christianity?*[78]

Thirty-four percent of the founder's quotes came directly from the Bible while another 60 percent were quotes of others who indirectly quoted scriptural principles. Our concept of three separate branches of government came from Isaiah 33:22 and the concept of separation of powers came from Jeremiah 17:9.

Throughout our history it has been apparent to the sincere seeker and in most cases even the insincere student of history that the providential hand of God has been on our nation from its very conception. *God's fingerprints can be found all over the place!*

THE DECLARATION OF INDEPENDENCE

The Declaration of Independence, according to constitutional attorney Michael Farris, was "the charter of our nation." It reveals what the majority of the colonists of the day believed – that they were establishing a new nation based soundly on the laws of God.

Commenting on the relationship of the Declaration of Independence to the Constitution, Farris declares, "By basing our right to be a free nation upon God's law, we were also saying (by implication) that we owed obedience to the law that allowed us to be a separate country. The last paragraph of the Declaration is the most important part, for it is the part which actually declared that the United States was a separate nation." Notice the wording of the Declaration:

> We, therefore, the Representatives of the United States of America, in General Congress, assembled, appealing to the Supreme Judge of the world for the rectitude of our intentions, do,

in the name and by the authority of the good people of these colonies, solemnly publish and declare, That these United Colonies are, and of Right ought to be Free and Independent States; that they are absolved from all allegiance to the British Crown, and that as Free and Independent States, that have the full power to levy war, conclude peace, contract alliances, establish Commerce, and to do all the other acts and things which Independent States may of right do.

And for the support of this Declaration, and with a firm reliance on the protection of divine Providence, we mutually pledge to each other our lives, our fortunes and our sacred honor.

Farris continues by saying: "The Declaration of the United States is our Charter. It is the legal document that made us a nation like all the other nations of the world. It doesn't tell us how we are going to run our country – that is what our Constitution does. In a corporation, the Charter is higher than the By-laws and the By-laws must be interpreted to be in agreement with the Declaration of the United States (more commonly known as the Declaration of Independence). The most important statement is that we want to operate under the laws of God." Why is all of this so important? Asks Farris, "Because today, when the courts are deciding what the Constitution means, they should remember our Charter – the Declaration of the United States. The Constitution doesn't specifically mention God, but then it doesn't have to because the Declaration is a higher document."[79]

The phrase "Laws of Nature and of Nature's God" derived from the Declaration of Independence are important for us to understand. The true definition of this phrase is found in William Blackstone's Law commentary, which was used in our nation until about 1920.[80] Our founding fathers quoted Blackstone often, and based much of their thinking upon his works. The commentary stated:

Man considered as a creature must necessarily be subject to the laws of his creator, for he is entirely a dependent being ... And consequently, a man depends absolutely upon his maker for everything, it is necessary that he should in all points conform to his maker's will. This will of his maker is called the law of nature.

This law of nature, being co-equal with mankind and dictated by God himself, is of course, superior in obligation to any other. It is binding over all the globe, in all countries', and at all times: no human laws are of any validity, if contrary to this...The doctrines thus delivered we call the revealed or divine law, and they are to be found in the holy scriptures...

Upon these two foundations, the law of nature and the law of revelation depend all human laws; that is to say, no human laws should be suffered to contradict these.[81]

Concerning the men who signed the Declaration of Independence, J. Eugene White asks, "Have you ever wondered what happened to the men who signed the Declaration of Independence?" Well, let's take a look:

Five signers were captured by the British as traitors and were tortured before they died. Twelve had their homes ransacked and burned. Two lost their sons in the Revolutionary Army. Another had two sons captured. Nine of the 56 fought and died from wounds and hardships.

What kind of men were they? 24 were lawyers and jurists, 11 were merchants, and 9 were farmers and large plantation owners, men of means, well educated. But they signed the Declaration of Independence knowing full well that the penalty would be death if they were captured.

They signed and pledged their lives, their fortunes and their sacred honor. Carter Braxton of Virginia, a wealthy planter and trader, saw his ships swept from the seas by the British navy. He sold his home and properties to pay his debts, and died in rags.

At the Battle of Yorktown, Thomas Nelson, Jr., noted that the British General Cornwallis had taken over the Nelson home for his headquarters. The owner quietly urged General Washington to open fire, which was done. The home was destroyed, and Nelson died bankrupt. Francis Lewis had his home and properties destroyed. The enemy jailed his wife, and she died within a few months.

John Hart was driven from his wife's bedside as she was dying. Their 13 children fled for their lives. His fields and gristmill were laid waste. For more than a year he lived in the forests and caves, returning home after the war to find his wife dead, his children vanished. A few weeks later he died from exhaustion and a broken heart.

Such were the sacrifices of the American Revolution. These were not wild-eyed, rabble-rousing ruffians. They were soft-spoken men of means and education. They had security, but they valued liberty more. Standing tall, straight, and unwavering, they pledged: "For the support of this declaration, with a firm reliance on the protection of the Divine Providence, we mutually pledge to each other, our lives, our fortunes, and our sacred honor."[82]

These men were great men of vision and valor. To these men, and thousands like them, we owe our freedom.

Our founding fathers sought divine wisdom in establishing this nation. As one author noted, "Reverently and humbly, the founders of our nation sought divine guidance in writing the creeds that became the guiding light of this new and independent country. The first sentence of the Declaration of Independence speaks of 'the Laws of Nature and of Nature's God;' and its final sentence expresses a 'firm reliance on the protection of Divine Providence.'" He continues by writing:

The Articles of Confederation, which preceded the Constitution, declare, "It has pleased the Great Governor of the world to incline the hearts of the legislatures we respectfully represent in Congress to approve of, and to authorize us to ratify, the said Articles of Confederation and perpetual union."

Engraved on the hearts of these Americans who had just won freedom from big government in England was the belief that a force greater than man had created the universe and in so doing had imposed certain natural laws, which would always prevail over man-made laws.

Here, for the first time in history, man called upon God to aid him in forming a government dedicated to the principle that each individual citizen, answerable ultimately only to God, should be free to work out his own spiritual and material destiny.[83]

THE BIBLE AND AMERICA

Many of the greatest leaders our nation has ever produced understood the importance of obedience to God's Word for our nation to prosper. John Quincy Adams said, "The first and almost the only book deserving of universal attention is the Bible." Former president Woodrow Wilson proclaimed the Bible as the "one supreme source of revelation of the meaning of life, the nature of God and spiritual nature and need of men. It is the only guide of life which really leads the spirit in the way of peace and salvation."

President Wilson understood the importance of the Bible, seeing it as "the one supreme source of revelation of the meaning of life" and "the only guide of life." President Calvin Coolidge understood the importance of God's Word as the "foundations of our society" and recognized that if we turned our back on Biblical principles, our society and our government" could not stand. President Coolidge said:

The foundations of our society and our government rest so much on the teachings of the Bible that it would be difficult to support them if faith in these teachings would cease to be practically universal in our country.[84]

Unfortunately, the history books have been revised and the fingerprints of God have been removed. Because of this, our nation has drifted off its course and has lost its sense of destiny. Historian Daniel Boorstin once wrote, "We have become a nation of short-term doomsayers. In a word, we have lost our sense of history. Without the materials of historical comparison, we are left with nothing but abstracts."[85]

Whether or not we are willing to recognize the importance Judeo-Christian values played in laying a "sure foundation" for this nation, the founding fathers did. The French historian Guizot once asked the American poet, James Russell Lowell, "How long will the American Republic endure?" Lowell, educated at Harvard College and Law School, answered, "As long as the ideas of the men who founded it continue to be dominant."[86] Concerning the Constitution, Daniel Webster said:

> When we speak of preserving the constitution, we mean not the paper on which it is written, but the spirit, which dwells in it. Government may lose all of the real character, its genius, its temper without losing its appearance. Republicanism, unless you guard it, will creep out of its case of parchment, like a snake out of its skin. You may look on a government, and see it possesses all the external modes of freedom, and yet finding nothing of the essence, the vitality, of freedom in it; just as you may contemplate an embalmed body, where art hath preserved proportion and form, amid nerves without action, and veins void of blood.

The only anti-Christian man of the founding era, Thomas Paine, best known for his laudable book *Common Sense*, which helped to kindle the War for Independence, later wrote an anti-Christian book, *Age of Reason*, in an attempt to discredit Christianity. Paine sent the book to our founding fathers. They all regarded the book with tremendous disdain and displeasure. Benjamin Franklin, one of only three founders (out of fifty-six signers of the Declaration) who wasn't a member of an orthodox Christian church responded to Paine's folly with these words:

> I have read over your manuscript with some attention. ... The consequence of printing this piece will be a great deal of odium drawn upon yourself, mischief to you, and no benefit to others. *He that spits into the wind spits in his own face. But were you to succeed, do you imagine any good would be done by it?* ... Think about how great a portion of mankind consists of weak and ignorant men and women, and of inexperienced, inconsiderate youth of both sexes, who have need of the motives of religion to restrain them from vice, to support their virtue, and to retain them in practice of it till it becomes habitual, which is the great point for its security. *And perhaps you are indebted to her originally, that is, to your religious education, for the habits of virtue upon which you now justly value yourself.*[87]

Franklin, though not a Christian himself understood that if Christianity were to be undermined, the moral foundations of our country would slip into oblivion. How dangerous it is for a nation to turn its back on God. Both the Holy Scriptures and the history textbooks remind us of this danger. As one author warned, "History is cluttered with the wreckage of nations that have become indifferent to God, and died."[88] Jim Nelson Black reinforces this warning, in his book, *When Nations Die*:

> No matter how far back you look, you will find that religion was always foundational to great societies ... Civilization arises from religion, and when the traditional religious beliefs of a nation are eroded, the nation dies.[89]

If we don't get back to our roots, our roots as a "Christian Nation," the erosion and eradication of our nation will become a reality and finality.

- CHAPTER 4 -

THE FOUNDATIONS HAVE BEEN DESTROYED

If the foundations be destroyed, what can the righteous do?

-Psalms 11:3

As both history and God's word attest, the foundations of a nation will determine the future of that nation. Former FBI director, J. Edgar Hoover in reviewing his fifty years in the FBI said, "Whether we like it or not the morals to which we subscribe as a people are vital for our survival as a free nation." For many years now, the foundations that once made this nation great have been viciously attacked, and they are eroding right before our eyes. The moral core of our nation is being eroded right before our eyes and at our expense. As author Carl Sommer reminds us:

> There are two ways to destroy a society: by overcoming it from without by the use of superior military might, or by overpowering it from within by encouraging such forces as will foster internal moral decay.[90]

As a nation we are perishing because we have drifted far from the foundational principles found in the Holy Scriptures and that the Founders laid down for us over 225 years ago. Because a nation's future is dependent upon its foundation, it is vital that we heed carefully the words of our Lord.

Matthew 7:26-27, "And every one that heareth these sayings of mine, and doeth them not, shall be likened unto a foolish man, which built his house upon the sand: And the rains descended, and the floods came, and the winds blew, and beat upon that house; and it fell: and great was the fall of it."

Notice the words, "and great was the fall of it." We have set ourselves up for a great fall because the foundation has been battered and chipped away over the years. For many years now, the foundations of this nation have been attacked from many different fronts, and by many different foes.

The pillars of this once great nation have been eroding away. We have now reached the point where the average American is left without a clear set of guidelines for living. Moral relativism reigns in America today! We have been left floundering in the mire of doubt, fear and indecision—a nation without a distinct and divine purpose.

Our faith gives meaning to life. Of course, the opposite is true. Our lack of Biblical faith results in a meaningless life and existence, not only for an individual—but also for a nation. To determine the faith of a nation, or the lack thereof, look to its institutions. The people, documents, institutions, educational establishments, courts, and halls of government will speak volumes regarding a nation's faith and its religious commitment.

For many years now, the foundations that once made this nation great have been viciously attacked, and are eroding right before our eyes. America's godly heritage has become, for the most part, "a fading memory" from a far off distant past. Not only have our foundations been attacked, they have been changed. That which once was the foundation of this great and glorious nation – God's Word – has been replaced by humanistic and socialistic pottage. On May 28, 1849, Robert C.

Winthrop, speaker of the Thirtieth Congress, issued this warning:

> The voice of experience and the voice of our own reason speak but one language.... Both unite in teaching us, that *men may as well build their houses upon the sand and expect to see them stand,* when the rains fall, and the winds blow, and the floods come, as to found free institutions upon any other basis than that morality and virtue, of which the Word of God is the only authoritative rule, and the only adequate sanction.
>
> All societies of men must be governed in some way or other. ... Men, in a word, must necessarily be controlled, either by a power within them, or by a power without them; either by the Word of God, or by the strong-arm of man; either by the Bible, or by the bayonet. It may do for other countries and other governments to talk about the State supporting religion. Here, under our own free institutions, it is Religion, which must support the State.[91]

In spite of the fact that a good portion of Americans still claim to be "Christians," and the "Bible is a perennial best seller," (with more Bibles being published and purchased in America than any other nation in the world); "the Bible has virtually disappeared," not only from American public schools but also from the public square.[92] The elimination of the Bible as the "rule of faith and practice" in the day in which we live has resulted in the repulsive renovation of our country.

We have all known for quite some time that our situation in America is "desperate," and that the foundational and traditional values that made this country great are deteriorating and being destroyed. The words of Aleksander Solzhenitsyn may describe our current situation best: "The situation is not dire, the situation is not threatening-the situation is catastrophic."

There is nothing like looking at the nation we love and seeing that our present situation is "catastrophic." For many of us, it seems hard to believe that we have drifted so far, from even the most basic traditional values that we once held near and dear. Just casually looking at the daily newspaper or watching the daily news can be depressing and discouraging. As a nation, we have traded that which was holy and right for that which is unholy and wrong.

As a nation, we have lost our sense of purpose and destiny. We have become the personification of an ailing giant who, "having exchanged his God-given Christian heritage for a bowl of humanistic Socialist pottage has lost his sense of destiny and purged his mind of any trace of morality."[93]

The values clarification programs have eliminated God, and have erased our godly heritage as a nation from the classroom textbooks. These textbooks, instituted in our schools over the past four or five decades, "have left our nation without a moral anchor," and without a compass to guide it into the way it should go – the result has been apathy, apostasy and anarchy!

OUR MORALS DETERMINE OUR MIGHT

The late Police Chief Parker, of the Los Angeles Police Department, also expressed pessimism about the future of our society. He said that he was "very much concerned" about the way in which things are going. He continued by saying:

> It is very hard for me to believe that our society can continue to violate all the fundamental rules of human conduct and expect to survive. I think I have to conclude that this civilization will destroy itself as others have before it. This leaves only one question-when?

We have now reached the point where the average American is left without a clear set of guidelines for living. We have been left floundering in the mire of doubt, fear and indecision – a nation without a distinct and divine purpose. As someone once said, "America is a nation which stands for nothing, but will fall for anything." Again Des Griffin had it right when he said:

> America today may be likened to a desperately sick man whose body is wracked with all kinds of deadly diseases. His eyesight and hearing are weak, his limbs are crippled with arthritis, his mental state is rapidly deteriorating, his heart is failing, and cancer is gnawing away at his vitals. Yet, dumbly and naively, he is frantically trying to persuade himself that all is well and that everything will work out all right in the end.[94]

We continue to convince ourselves that "everything's all right," but as historian Arnold Toynbee once said, "Moral decay from within has destroyed most of the world's great civilizations." If moral decay has destroyed others, it will destroy America.

Author Kevin Swanson is very pointed in his declaration; "There has been no break in this constant 100-year crushing of the Christian moral structure in our culture." He continues by stating:

> There was no Reagan conservative revolution. There never was a reduction in the Planned Parenthood grants. There was never a reduction in the number of pro-death, pro-homosexual justices on the U.S. Supreme Court. *Christians have made no progress with their governments in the United States.* Ignore the rhetoric.
>
> Look at the net effect of Christianity in America over the last 100 years. A cursory examination of the facts would find that there were 1.3 million abortions in 1977 and 1.6 million abortions in 1992. That is 0% progress. Zero! We would have left a greater impression if we placed our finger in a cup of water and pulled it out.[95]

Our enemies have known that in order to have complete control of the "masses," they must anesthetize the people against feeling the tyranny by encouraging them into immorality, uncontrolled lust and sin.

Freedom is only possible "when there is a strong moral force within that restrains us and strong civil laws against the crimes of adultery, rape, theft, and murder [and] the socialists do all they can to tear this moral force away."[96] Remember what Winthrop declared:

> Men, in a word, must necessarily be controlled either by a power within them, or by a power without them; either by the word of God, or by the strong arm of man, either by the Bible, or the bayonet.

GOD IS DEAD

"God is Dead," announced the *Time* magazine in its April 8, 1966, cover story. As far as the "liberal elite" was concerned, God was no longer real or relevant, but needed to be replaced. In other words, this generation had replaced God by simply declaring Him dead. Listen to the words of one author who asks a few thought-provoking questions:

> How did we reach such a point that a nation founded in part on presuppositions of God's existence would then deny that existence and any accountability to Him? Was it accidental or was it deliberate? Rather than God "dying," did the culture commit homicide (or suicide)?[97]

He continues by saying, "Despair amidst an endless search for significance. It is the station at which the sixties generation has, for the most part, arrived. They seem always to be seeking, but never able to find knowledge of the truth."[98]

It would not be difficult to understand why the people of God, in America today, would cry out, "Where is the God of Elijah?" Like the children of Israel during the time of Jeremiah, present day America has committed two evils. First, we have forsaken the true and living God, the God of the Bible, Who is the true "Fountain of Living Waters." Second, we have replaced Him with "cisterns, broken cisterns, that can hold no water." Over the past four to five decades as a nation, we have been guilty of exchanging the truth of God's eternal Word, the Living Waters, for the corrupt cisterns that cannot hold water and cannot truly satisfy.

> *Jeremiah 2:11-13, "Hath a nation changed their gods, which are yet not gods? But My people have changed their glory for that which doth not profit. ... For My people have committed two evils; they have forsaken Me the fountain of living waters, and hewed them out cisterns, broken cisterns, that can hold no water.*

Because of our departure from God there is "a famine in the land." This famine is not one of physical "bread, nor a thirst for water, but of hearing the words of the Lord." Our departure from God as a nation has resulted in the acceptance of the moldy and stale bread of humanism, secularism and atheism – which have resulted in paganism.

A humanistic and/or atheistic worldview sees man as the center of all reality. Archibald Alexander was right when he said, "Men may be induced to abandon their old religion and to adopt a new one; but they never can remain long free from all religion. Take away one object of worship and they will soon attach themselves to another. If unhappily they lose the knowledge of the true God, they will set up gods of their own invention or receive them from others."[99] In the words of one author, "By rejecting God's interpretation of reality, man believes he can interpret reality independently, not realizing the consequences of distortion due to his own inherent limitations."

From Moses to Abraham Lincoln to Alexander Solzhenitsyn have come warnings of the severe consequences to nations that forget and forsake God. "The proof that they were right is found in the carcasses of long-dead cultures and philosophies that are strewn along the road of history. ... The unraveling of nations occurs when man attempts to topple God and replace His authority with our own"[100] Cal Thomas rightly perceives, "The decline of American culture, hastened by spiritual deficiency, continues unabated in the nineties. But the infection began in the sixties, and those who caught it continue to afflict the rest of us."[101]

FORGETTING GOD

Beware that thou forget not the LORD thy God, in not keeping his commandments, and his judgments, and his statutes, which I command thee this day: Lest when thou hast eaten and art full, and hast built goodly houses, and dwelt therein; And when thy herds and thy flocks multiply, and thy silver and thy gold is multiplied, and all that thou hast is multiplied; Then thine heart be lifted up, and thou forget the LORD thy God, which brought thee forth out of the land of Egypt, from the house of bondage. - Deuteronomy 8:11-14

As we mentioned in our book *Temples of Darkness*, the objective of much of public education, was, still is, and will always be, to get God out of the picture. In this they have succeeded. In 1983, the Russian, Aleksander Solzhenitsyn, winner of the 1970 Nobel Prize for Literature, gave an address in London in which he attempted to explain why so much evil had befallen his people:

Over a half a century ago, while I was still a child, I recall hearing a number of old people offer the following explanation for the great disasters that had befallen Russia: 'Men have forgotten God; that's why all this has happened.' Since then I have spent well nigh 50 years working on the history of our revolution; in the process I have read hundreds of books, collected hundreds of testimonies, and have already contributed eight volumes of my own toward the effort of clearing away the rubble left by that upheaval. But if I were asked today to formulate as concisely as possible the main cause of the ruinous revolution that swallowed up some sixty million of our people, I could not put it more accurately than to repeat; *"Men have forgotten God; that's why all this has happened."*[102]

As we mentioned in *Temples of Darkness*, there is a very subtle, systematic, and satanic strategy now in place to create, here in America, a socialistic society that has forgotten God and His Word. To be frank with you, they are not even being very subtle about it anymore. Abraham Lincoln saw this coming well over 100 years ago. Lincoln proclaimed a national Day of Prayer and Fasting, Humiliation and Prayer (boy, would the A.C.L.U. have a time with this one), in which he said:

The recipients of the choicest bounties of heaven, we have been preserved, these many years, in peace and prosperity. We have grown in numbers, wealth and power, as no other nation has ever grown. But we have forgotten God. We have forgotten the gracious hand, which preserved us in peace ... we have vainly imagined in the deceitfulness of our hearts, that all these blessings were produced by some superior wisdom and virtue of our own. Intoxicated with unbroken success, we have become too self-sufficient ...too proud...it behooves us, then to confess our national sins, and pray for clemency and forgiveness.[103]

As a nation we have forgotten God, and because of this we are quickly becoming a nation of infidels and idolaters. The fiery zealot and patriot, Patrick Henry, vehemently reminds us what happens when a nation forgets God. The born-again Henry said, "Bad men cannot make good citizens. It is impossible that a nation of infidels or idolaters should be a nation of free men. It is when a people forget God that tyrants forge their chains."[104]

For most of our history, our leaders have understood that "the survival of our republic depended upon the virtue of its citizens."[105] Former American statesman Daniel Webster may have said it best, citing:

> Lastly, our ancestors established their system of government on morality and religious sentiment. Moral habits, they believed, cannot safely be trusted on any other foundation than religious principle, nor any government be secure which is not supported by moral habits.... ***Whatever makes men good Christians makes them good citizens.***[106]

Notice what Webster said, "[O]ur ancestors established their system of government on **morality** and **religious sentiment,**" this was the foundation laid by our founders. Like Daniel Webster, our Founding Fathers knew full and well "Whatever makes men good Christians makes them good citizens." Naturally, the opposite is true!

God help us to get back to seeing our present day situation through the "eyes of God," rather than the eyes of man. We must understand that "if man's dependence upon God for knowledge is considered optional, then God's view of the world is also considered optional. By rejecting God's view of the world,"[107] we become free to create our own worldview and in due time will reap the consequences.

> ***Galatians 6:7-8a,*** *"Be not deceived; God is not mocked: for whatsoever a man soweth, that shall he also reap. For he that soweth to his flesh shall of the flesh reap corruption..."*

> ***Proverbs 22:8,*** *"He that soweth iniquity shall reap vanity: and the rod of his anger shall fail."*

Hosea 10:7, "For they have sown the wind, and they shall reap the whirlwind..."

Romans 2:8, "But unto them that are contentious, and do not obey the truth, but obey unrighteousness, indignation and wrath."

No matter how sincere, and no matter how seemingly "constructive;" any worldview formed independent of the Holy Scriptures "makes man an idol worshipper" who has exchanged the truth of God's Word for the lies of this present world.

Romans 1:22-23 & 25, "Professing themselves to be wise, they became fools, And changed the glory of the uncorruptible God into an image made like to corruptible man ... Who changed the truth of God into a lie, and worshipped and served the creature more than the Creator, who is blessed for ever. Amen."

Our freedoms are slipping down the drain as we have lost sight of the One Who makes and will keep us free, the Lord Jesus Christ. One preacher said it well when he proclaimed, "If God doesn't judge America, He owes Sodom and Gomorrah an apology." The Quaker, and founder of Pennsylvania, William Penn, understood the inevitable result of a nation that forgets God. He said, "If we will not be governed by God, we will be ruled by tyrants."[108] One of our founding fathers, Noah Webster, made it very clear:

> The religion, which has introduced civil liberty, is the religion of Christ and His apostles ... [t]his is genuine Christianity, and to this we owe our free Constitutions of Government. The moral principles precepts contained in the Scriptures ought to form the basis of all our civil constitutions and laws.... All the miseries and evils, which men suffer from vice, crime, ambition, injustice, oppression, slavery and war, proceed from their despising or neglecting the precepts found in the Bible.[109]

THE DECHRISTIANIZATION OF AMERICA

In Bork's book *Slouching Towards Gomorrah*, he offers a prophetic and unprecedented view of our American culture in decline, a nation in such serious moral trouble that its very foundation is crumbling before our eyes. Concerning former president Clinton, Bork writes:

> Thirty years ago, Clinton's behavior would have been absolutely disqualifying. Since the 1992 election, the public has learned far more about what is known, euphemistically, as the "character issue." Yet none of this appears to affect Clinton's popularity. It is difficult not to conclude that something about our moral perceptions and reactions has changed profoundly. If that change is permanent, the implication for our future is bleak.[110]

Within just a matter of a few decades the sure foundation, set in place by our Puritan forefathers and patriotic founding fathers, was being replaced by the shifting sand and new "winds of doctrine," formulated in the minds of men who denied the validity of God's Word, and defied the authority of God's will over mankind. As Bible believers, we must acknowledge the forces that are devoted to destroy our faith, our families, and the foundational values upon which this nation was birthed and has blossomed for over 200 years.

Gradually socialistic, humanistic, and atheistic philosophies have crept in to the "way of life" of many Americans today. What we are witnessing in America today is "trickle down" indifference and immorality. These putrid philosophies have "trickled down" from the "high places" in our elected representation, in our entertainment field, and in our educational systems. Concerning the gradual takeover of our nation, Patrick Buchanan voices the same truth that many others have said, when answering the question, "How could our faith be uprooted?

> Gramsci's answer–a "long march" through the institutions. The Marxists must cooperate with the progressives to capture the institutions that shaped the souls of the young: schools, colleges, movies, music, arts, and the new mass media that came uncensored into every home, radio, and, after Gramsci's death, television. Once the cultural institutions were captured, a united Left could begin the de-Christianization of the West. When, after several generations, this was accomplished, the West could no longer be the West, but another civilization altogether, and control of the state would inevitably follow control of the culture.[111]

THE ENLIGHTENED HUMANIST

Concerning humanistic philosophies that are permeating our nation, Dr. Francis Schaffer, the Christian philosopher, once declared, "All roads from humanism lead to chaos." Unfortunately, as LaHaye writes, "it usually takes a generation or two before the chaos becomes apparent."[112]

The Enlightenment's success in eighteenth century Europe, writes one author, "paved the way for three of the most destructive philosophies ever devised by the secularist brain: evolution, Marxism, and humanistic psychology." As is well known, by a casual study of history, "Charles Darwin, Karl Marx, Sigmund Freud, and others who shared their views have produced more human suffering through government-sponsored secularism than all the previous evils known to man combined."[113]

When the founders gathered in Philadelphia to write the Constitution, "they had ample evidence that unrestrained democracy led to anarchy." Such conditions had caused the religiously minded leaders and citizens to "choose delegates who had a deep commitment to the religious roots of the colonists who established this country."[114] Those in attendance for this historic occasion were selected "for their deep commitment to Puritan and Calvinistic doctrine, as well as for other political considerations."

As LaHaye writes, their "goal was not to establish a democracy in which every man does what is right in his own eyes," but our founders "formulated a representative form of government based on divinely inspired law."[115]

Our founders laid the foundation for a government to become "one nation under God," and never intended for it to become a secular state. It is interesting to note that the "first college chartered by atheists, was not founded until 1861, or seventy-two years after the founding of America."[116]

As Gary DeMar stated in his book *God and Government*, "Some authority, whether it be God or man, is used as a reference point for all enacted laws. If a political system rejects one authority, it adopts another. If a biblical moral system is not being legislated, then an immoral system is being legislated. Any moral system that does not put Jesus Christ at its center, denies Christ."[117]

Our country is being influenced and infected each day with various "spiritual viruses." This attack is infecting every aspect of our nation; the viruses have infected all of us to some degree. These viruses are undermining the spiritual foundations of our faith, and they are challenging our value system and changing the way we look at society as a whole. As one author declared:

> Oh, then mental and moral and spiritual "fall-out" that has polluted and perverted millions of young people in our Western

world! We are reminded of the plague of Black Death in Europe in the 14th century. That plague, so very contagious and accompanied by fever and prostration, was usually fatal.

Fleas from infected rats were the carriers of that awful scourge. But today we have a polluting plague worse than the plague of Black Death, a plague carrying the brood of infected moral rats-the writers of pornography, the promoters of sex literature, the pushers of drugs, the peddlers of dope. And what might we say of the professors and philosophers who peddle atheistic evolution and God-hating communism and Christ-denying education? Was not China thus taken over by the power of the polluting pen?

We need to, as a nation, get back to the foundations upon which this nation was founded. Former president Herbert Hoover, in 1943, issued this statement, "Menaced by collectivist trends, we must seek revival of our strength in the *spiritual foundations* which are the bedrock of our republic. Democracy is the outgrowth of the religious conviction of the sacredness of every human life. On the religious side, its highest embodiment is the Bible; on the political side, the Constitution."[118] President Hoover also reminds us, "The whole inspiration of our civilization springs from the teachings of Christ and the lessons of the prophets. To read the Bible for these fundamentals is a necessity of life."[119]

SEPARATION OF CHURCH AND STATE

As one author put it, "There is great confusion in our day for Christians as well as non-Christians – regarding the relationship of Church and state."[120] Far too many of God's people have been duped into believing that "religion" is not to be a part of our political system, our public schools and/or the public square. To this they "point to the First Amendment of the Constitution for their ideological viewpoint."[121] A great majority of Christians today have bought into the supposed "separation of Church and State" and in doing so, we have literally handed over our communities and our culture to a secular and satanic influence.

In the past generation there has been a systematic effort to erase any evidence of Christianity in public life. Hiding behind the guise of *"pluralism,* a hostile *secularism* attacks any expression of Christian ideas or beliefs in public," and all of this under the fallacy of "separation of Church and State." Dr. James Kennedy is right on target when he states:

> The separation of Church and State, which is not even in our Constitution, has now been misconstrued to mean separation of *God* from the State. Thus, the so-called "constitutional separation of Church and State" has turned the establishment clause of the First Amendment into a search-and-destroy mission for any vestige of Christianity in the public arena.[122]

In a "Sermon on National Sins," James H. Thornwell addressed the idea of separating Christianity from the State. Even though it was preached more than 100 years ago, it is extremely applicable today. Thornwell rightly said:

> When we insist upon the religious character of the State, we are not to be understood as recommending or favoring a Church Establishment. To have a religion is one thing, to have a Church Establishment is another; and perhaps the most effectual way of extinguishing the religious life of a State is to confine the expression of it to the forms and peculiarities of a single sect [denomination]. The Church and State, as visible institutions are entirely distinct, and neither can usurp the province of the other without injury to both.
>
> ... The State realizes its religious character through the religious character of its subjects; and a State is and ought to be Christian, because all its subjects are and ought to be determined by the principles of the Gospel. As every legislator is bound to be a Christian man, he has no right to vote for any laws, which are

inconsistent with the teachings of Scriptures. He must carry his Christian conscience into the halls of legislation.[123]

As Gary DeMar stated in his book *God and Government*: "Some authority, whether it be God or man, is used as a reference point for all enacted laws. If a political system rejects one authority, it adopts another. If a biblical moral system is not being legislated, then an immoral system is being legislated. Any moral system that does not put Jesus Christ at its center, denies Christ."[124]

The phrase "a wall of separation between Church and State" had its origin in a letter written in 1802 by Thomas Jefferson to the Danbury Baptists who were concerned that the Congregational denomination was going to be made the national religion. As DeMar states, "Our courts have substituted Thomas Jefferson's misunderstood phrase for the true meaning of the First Amendment."[125] Thomas Jefferson, because of this phrase, has become the "poster boy" of atheists, humanists and socialists of our day, in spite of the fact that Jefferson had nothing to do with writing the Constitution (he was in France at the time), and in spite of the fact the phrase itself has been taken out of its true context.

The "poster boy" himself once said, "I consider the government of the United States as interdicted [prohibited] by the Constitution from intermeddling with religious institutions, their doctrines, discipline, or exercises." Mr. Jefferson understood that the First Amendment was to keep the State out of Church affairs not the Church out of State affairs. Jefferson continued with this thought by saying, "This results not only from the provision that no law shall be made respecting an establishment or free exercise of religion, but from that also which reserves to the states the powers not delegated to the general government. It must then rest with the states, as far as it can be in any human authority…"[126]

As John Whitehead declared, "Historically understood, the First Amendment would read: 'The federal government shall make no law having anything to do with supporting a single church, or government preference of one Christian creed or denomination over another' … The First Amendment, therefore, provides freedom for religion, not from religion. The states by this amendment were afforded that freedom in the area of religion."[127]

As Dr. Kennedy writes, "The turning point in American jurisprudence in church-state matters was the 1947 *Everson v. Board of Education* decision. Justice Hugo Black applied for the first time the 'separation of Church and State' concept to the First Amendment."[128] Even the liberal *Time* magazine pointed out in 1996, "That ruling marked *a sharp separationist turn in court thinking*. It unleashed a torrent of litigation that continues to flood courtrooms years later. And in a succession of cases, the court drew the line ever more strictly."[129]

Through the years, this false understanding of the First Amendment "came to gain wide circulation, so much so, that the average person today most likely thinks that the Constitution even teaches the separation of Church and State,"[130] which of course, it doesn't. It is very interesting to note that between 1941-1971 – when many of the "liberal" decisions made by the highest court in our land were made – the court was stacked with men who were members of the Masonic Order. These men and their philosophies controlled our U.S. Supreme Court, and drastically transformed our society, especially concerning the fallacy of "separation of Church and State." As Paul Fisher reminds us that the "goal of Masonry has always been to change our nation from a Christian country to a secular society. They have accomplished their objective."[131]

Paul Fisher's book, *Behind the Lodge Door*, is an excellent source of information on Freemasonry. Fisher informs us that between 1941-1971, Masons dominated the Supreme Court "in ratios ranging from 5 to 4 (1941-1946, 1969-1971) to 8 to 1 (1949-1956). During the 30-year period, the Court erected 'a wall' separating things religious from things secular. It was an epoch when prayer and Bible reading were deracinated from public education." Fisher continues by stating, "Masons have succeeded in having their religion dominate American society."[132]

It wasn't long before this fallacy struck in the High Court again, this time under the Warren Court. The infamous school prayer decisions in 1962 and 1963, *Engle v. Vitale*, *Abington v. Schempp*, and *Murray v. Curlett* officially "kicked God out of school without the hope of a reprieve." Of course, our schools (see *Temples of Darkness*) and society have never been the same. While the fallacy of "separation of Church and State" cannot be found in our Constitution, it can be found in the constitution of the old Soviet Union. Soviet Union's Constitution reads as follows:

> In order to insure to citizens freedom of conscience, the Church in the U.S.S.R. is separated from the State, and the school from the Church. Freedom of religious worship and freedom of anti-religious propaganda is recognized for all citizens.[133]

Author J.M. O'Neill wrote in *Religion and Education Under the Constitution*:

> If the American people have ever adopted the principle of complete separation of Church and state, we would find evidence of it in the federal Constitution, in the acts of Congress, or in the

constitutions of the several states. ***There is no such evidence in existence***.[134]

As one historian and author declared, "It was never the purpose of the Constitution to give religious content to the nation. Rather, the Constitution was an instrument whereby already existing religious values of the nation could be protected and perpetuated."[135] Of course, those already "existing religious values" were Christian values. The only way that the modern secularist can come to the conclusion that our founders intended for the United States to be a "secular state," is to be selective, very selective, in their historical study.

Timothy Dwight, president and professor at Yale College from 1795 to his death in 1817, made it clear, " Religion and liberty are the meat and drink of the body politic. Withdraw one of them and it languishes, consumes, and dies. If indifference to either, at any time, becomes the prevailing character of the people, one half of their motives to vigorous defense is lost, and the hopes of their enemies are proportionally increased." Dwight went on to say:

> Without religion we may possibly retain the freedom of savages, bears, and wolves, but not the freedom of New England. If our religion were gone, our state of society would perish with it and nothing would be left worth defending. Our children, of course, if not ourselves, would be prepared, as the ox for the slaughter to become victims of conquest, tyranny, and atheism…[136]

Concerning the relationship of the church and the state, A.A. Hodges once wrote:

> If the Church languishes, the State cannot be in health; and if the State rebels against its Lord and King, the Church cannot enjoy his favour. If the Holy Ghost is withdrawn from the Church, He is not present in the State; and if he, the only "Lord, the Giver of

Life," be absent, then all order is impossible, and the elements of society lapse backward to primeval night and chaos...

I charge you, the citizens of the United States, afloat on your wide sea of politics, THERE IS ANOTHER KING, ONE JESUS; THE SAFETY OF THE STATE CAN BE SECURED ONLY IN THE WAY OF HUMBLE AND WHOLE-SOULED LOYALTY TO HIS PERSON AND OF OBEDIENCE TO HIS LAW.[137]

Associate Justice of the United States Supreme Court Joseph Story once wrote:

The real object of the First Amendment was not countenance, much less to advance, Mohammedanism, or Judaism, or infidelity, by prostrating Christianity; but to exclude all rivalry among Christian sects (denominations), and to prevent any national ecclesiastical establishment, which should give to a hierarchy the exclusive patronage of the national government.

It thus cuts off the means of religious persecution (the vice and pest of former ages), and of the subversion of the rights of conscience in matters of religion, which had been trampled upon almost from the days of the Apostles to the present age...

Probably at the time of the adoption of the Constitution, and of the first amendment to it ... the general, if not the universal, sentiment in America was that Christianity ought to receive encouragement from the State, so far as was not incompatible with the previous rights of conscience and the freedom of religious worship. An attempt to level all religions and to make it a matter of state policy to hold all in utter indifference would have created universal disapprobation, if not universal indignation.[138]

Therefore, to see the state as the only governing institution "is destructive of liberty and of life."[139] The Constitution guarantees our liberties – our freedom of speech, press, assembly, and religion, our right to choose our leaders and our right to fair trials. Half of mankind lacks these liberties; our desire to keep them also justifies our vigilance. If our adversaries have their way, a constitutional convention for the purpose of "revising" the constitution, will take place.

A few years after the founding of our nation, Jedediah Morse, the father of American geography, wrote: "Whenever the pillars of Christianity shall be overthrown, our present republican form of government, and all the blessings that flow from them, must fall with them."[140] Not only will this nation fall, but "great will be the fall." In the words of Dr. Edwin Lutzer, "Not until all is lost will many awake to the painful reality that America as we once knew it is gone."

THE FOUNDATIONS HAVE BEEN DESTROYED

"... [T] he United States system of national popular education will be the most efficient and wide instrument for the propagation of atheism the world has ever seen ... I am as sure as I am of the fact of Christ's reign that a comprehensive and centralized system of national education, separated from religion, as is now commonly proposed, will prove the most appalling enginery for the propagation of anti-Christian and atheistic unbelief, and of anti-social nihilistic ethics, individual social and political institution which this sin-rent world has ever seen."

-A.A. Hodges

- CHAPTER 5 -

AMERICA'S TROJAN HORSE: "PUBLIC" EDUCATION

According to ancient legend, the fierce Mycenaean's destroyed the city of Troy on the coast of Asia Minor after a ten-year siege. Legend has it that the deciding victory came after the Mycenaean's pretended to depart for home, leaving behind a large wooden horse (the infamous Trojan Horse) with soldiers hidden inside. When the curious Trojans brought the horse inside their city walls, the hidden soldiers came out and opened the gates, allowing their comrades to enter and destroy the city.

Since the beginning of our nation there has been a siege to take control of our nation. For many years, the siege was small, a battle here and a battle there, but for the most part, unsuccessful.

In the early part of the nineteenth century, under the leadership of Horace Mann and others, a "Trojan Horse" was placed in our country. The "enemies of the cross," and enemies of our constitutional republic, to open the doorway for all type of evil, have used this Trojan Horse, our present day government-run public school system. As a matter of fact, this has been the objective since the beginning. In a letter written in 1829 to Fabian Socialist Robert Dale Owen, we find these words:

> The great object was to get rid of Christianity and to convert our churches into halls of science. The plan was to establish ...

89

> national schools from which all religion was to be excluded, in which nothing was to be taught but such a knowledge as is verifiable by the senses, and to which all parents were to be compelled by law to send their children....[141]

Owen failed in his attempt to start the first "socialist" community in the United States. His failure in New Harmony was a time of great learning. The great lesson learned by Owen and his followers was that *education and indoctrination had to precede the creation of a socialist and secular society*. In other words, the American people were not yet ready to accept socialism, and from that moment on, they decided that they would promote national public education as the preliminary step to socialism. Owen realized that the parents were the primary force in teaching children the values of the society, and *this practice had to cease if socialism was to succeed in the United States*.

As author Dr. John Coleman so duly noted, "Perhaps in no other of their fields of endeavor to Socialize America did their indirect, stealthy, furtive methodology succeed nearly as much as it did in Fabian Socialism's long march to capture the educational system of this nation."[142]   Coleman continues with this thought by writing:

> The Socialists took over Yale, Harvard, Columbia and many other colleges, held to be of direct service to Socialism. They were to be the future educational centers and "finishing schools" for Socialists in America as Oxford and Cambridge are for the Fabian Society in England.[143]

In 1976, the year of our nation's bicentennial, education's progressive educational "high priests finally succeeded in their long-standing struggle to shift schools away from academics and scholarship to guardianship and socialization."[144] These "educrats" (educational bureaucrats) live by the philosophy as noted by renowned behavioral eugenicist Paul Popenoe, and claim "the educational system should be a sieve, through which all of the children of the country are passed."[145] Regrettably, millions upon millions of our citizens have passed through the sieve, having their values and vision changed, becoming "philosophically" and "politically" correct.

PUBLIC EDUCATION'S UNHOLY TRINITY

"I think the most important factor moving us towards a secular society has been the educational factor. Our schools may not teach Johnny how to read properly but the fact that Johnny is in school until he is sixteen tends toward the elimination of religious superstition..." - Humanist Author, Paul Blanchard

Mr. Blanchard helps us to understand the "true" purpose of education in our government-run school systems. The objective of much of today's educational process has the purpose of "secularizing" our society and eliminating religious superstition. The ultimate goal of secular education is to *redefine our values*, and *redesign our institutions of learning* with the goal of *reconstructing a new society*, one that has forgotten God and His Word.

Men like Horace Mann, John Dewey, George Counts, B.F. Skinner, Harold Rugg and Carl Rogers, along with a host of other deceived and demented philosophers of perversion, believed in using the government-run school system as a tool for "social regeneration" to change "the face" of our country. Remember what Harold Rugg wrote in his book *The Great Technology:*

A new public mind is to be created. How? Only by creating tens of millions of individual minds and welding them into a new social mind. Old stereotypes must be broken up and new climates of opinion formed in the neighborhoods of America ... *through the schools of the world, we shall disseminate a new conception of government – one that will embrace all the activities of men ...* [146]

"A new public mind, millions of individual minds being welded into a new social mind, old stereotypes must be broken up." Folks, this sounds like a serious case of brainwashing to me. Not only are we talking about brainwashing, but also these promoters of socialism have been, and are still purposely filling the minds of our children with lies. It's interesting that he would mention "a new conception of government (from a republic to a socialistic democracy) and "embracing all the activities of men." Did I hear someone say "tolerance"?

Listen to the words of Norman Thomas, a socialist and member of the *A.C.L.U.*, who boldly told the world:

> The American people will never knowingly adopt socialism, but under the name of liberalism, they will adopt every fragment of the socialist program until one day *America will be a socialist nation without ever knowing how it happened.*"[147]

In the words of Paul Mantoux, "*the builder of this new world must be education ...* Plainly, the first step in the case of each country is to train an elite to think, feel, and act internationally."[148] Can anyone say "New World Order?"

Author and syndicated writer Cal Thomas reminds us that there was once a "general agreement on what students should be taught and what truth was and how it could be discovered. But education became another tool of sixties activists to indoctrinate this and future generations in their failed philosophy, lifestyles, and worldview. Schools were rapidly transformed into laboratories in which human guinea pigs were *inoculated with a philosophy alien to this country*."[149]

The unholy trinity that is being pushed on a daily basis in our government-run school system is socialism, humanism, and atheism. Of course, a steady diet of these three eventually results in unashamed paganism. What parents in America need to understand, and we did our best to convey this in our book *Temples of Darkness*, is that the basis of today's school crisis is the conflict between socialism, humanism, atheism and the traditional American value system based upon God's Word.

Our government-run school system has been thoroughly reconstructed, with a new mission statement. It has gone from being the foundational pillars in the building of our nation, to what is nothing more than incubators of immorality and indecency. As someone has said, "When we look at education today we see a situation that is very encouraging, even inspiring – to our enemies! The creators of a new 'social mind' have done a thorough job."

The new faith that is taught in our schools today is the religion of secular humanism. Listen to these words found in the *Humanist* magazine, which says unashamedly:

> **The battle for humankind's future must be waged and won in the public school classroom** by teachers who correctly perceive themselves as proselytizers of a new faith ... These teachers must embody the same selfless dedication as the most rabid fundamentalist preachers, for they will be the ministers of another sort, utilizing a classroom instead of a pulpit *to convey humanist values* in whatever subject they teach, regardless of the educational level – preschool, day care, or large state university. The classroom must and will become an arena of conflict between the old and the new – *the rotting corpse of Christianity, together with its adjacent evils and misery, and the new faith of humanism.*[150]

This guy sounds pretty radical, doesn't he? In the same manner that our preachers use the pulpit to influence and inspire men, women and children to live for Christ, these "ministers of **another sort**" are using classroom podiums to influence young people into a life of secular humanistic thinking. The schools have become effective instruments of indoctrination into a new value system. Whose values will win out? With children spending thirty to thirty-five hours per week, nine months per year for twelve or thirteen years under the influences of this ungodly garbage, is it any wonder we lose so many?[151] Author Cal Thomas reminds us that the humanist, for the purpose of experimentation and indoctrination, is using schools, when he declares that:

> The Humanist left knows the only way it can create substantial numbers of ideological and social robots eager to follow in their failed footsteps is to imprison substantial numbers of children in government schools where they are force-fed liberal ideology ... at taxpayer's expense.[152]

The humanists are not ashamed to admit the relationship between government-run schooling and humanism in the battle for our nation. Listen to the words of humanist Charles Potter:

> **Education is the most powerful ally of humanism**, and every American public school is a school of humanism. What can the theistic Sunday school, meeting for an hour a week, and teaching a fraction of the children, do to stem the tide of a five-day program of humanistic teaching?[153]

In answer to Potter's question, I would have to answer, not much! This is the reason we are losing so many of our young people. Yes, they may still attend our churches, out of habit, but are they really walking with God? Do they really believe that God's Word is the absolute truth? On the other hand, are they becoming indifferent, ignorant, and immoral like the rest of the world around them? Are they seeking after God or are they seeking after gold? Are they living lives that are pure or lives that are perverse?

The philosophy of humanism is anti-Bible and anti-family. As humanist Dr. Reginald Lourie wrote in **Marriage and the Family,** "Some opponents of Humanism have accused us of wishing to overthrow the Traditional Christian Family. They are right. That is exactly what we intend to do." Lourie makes it very clear "schools must begin to provide adequately for the emotional and moral development of children ... the school ... must assume a direct responsibility for the attitudes and values of child development."

Through a good portion of our history, Americans have had an almost undying faith in the school system to preserve, protect, and promote our republic. For the most part, at least humanly speaking, this faith had been well rewarded. There has never been a country whose educational system has served as many students as successfully as ours has. However, this faith is now presently in a system that is *failing* and *floundering* in regard to academic and character training.

A THREAT TO OUR NATIONAL SECURITY

In this Commission's view, the inadequacies of our systems of research and education pose a greater threat to U.S. national security over the next quarter century than any other potential conventional war that we might imagine.[154]

As we documented in our book *Temples of Darkness,* which is very obvious for the average American citizen, our schools have been drastically failing to accomplish what we have long felt they should. Without a doubt, our public schools are in trouble. This is a well-documented fact. Listen to these words from the April 1983 National Commission on Excellence in Education's historic report, *A Nation at Risk*, which said:

> The educational foundations of our society are presently being eroded by a rising tide of mediocrity that threatens our very future as a nation and as a people ... If an unfriendly foreign power had attempted to impose on America the mediocre educational performance that exists today, we might well have viewed it as an *act of war*. As it stands, we have allowed this to happen to ourselves ... we have, in effect, been committing an act of unthinking, unilateral educational disarmament.[155]

An *"act of war,"* now that is a strong indictment against our educational establishment, but it is an accurate one. Those words were written over fifteen years ago, but things have not improved at all. To be frank, things have worsened! Countless statistics, studies and special reports reveal that our school systems are not performing nearly up to par. Listen to the words penned in the *Washington Times* which confirm that this system is still mediocre at best:

> The fundamental indictment that came out of the [*Nation at Risk*] report was that kids weren't learning enough. Fifteen years later we're still saying that kids in this country aren't learning enough and their academic performance is still mediocre.[156]

A report released February 15, 2001 by the U.S. Commission on National Security calls the deficiencies in American math and science education *"threats to national security,"* which must be addressed immediately to protect the nation from "distinctly new dangers." The report continued with these frightening words:

> In this Commission's view, the inadequacies of our systems of research and education pose a greater threat to U.S. national security over the next quarter century than any other potential conventional war that we might imagine.[157]

Why are government-run schools "a greater threat to the U.S. national security?" How can the school systems of America be viewed as declaring war on America? The answer is simple: Government-run education has subtly undermined all that this nation was founded upon – beginning with God, the Bible, and our Constitutional republic.

The schools today are no longer simply in the business of instructing our children, but they have become involved with indoctrinating and shaping a new society – a secular and socialist society that has "forgotten God," and forsaken the foundations laid down by our founding fathers. A common thread running over the past sixty-five to seventy years was that "the purpose of education would be to focus on ... the student's behavior according to the preconceived model approved by government social engineers known as 'change agents.'"[158]

TEMPLES OF DARKNESS

"...I am very much afraid that schools will prove to be the great gates of hell unless they diligently labor in explaining the Holy Scriptures ... engraving them in the hearts of the youth. I advise no one to place his child where the Scriptures do not reign paramount. Every institution in which men are not increasingly occupied with the Word of God must become corrupt." - Martin Luther

The protestant reformer Martin Luther was right. Any institution that neglects God and His Word will become corrupt to the core, and filled with darkness. We are reminded, on what seems to be a daily basis, of the cancerous corruption that is eating away at the very core of our society – our government-run public school system. Samuel Blumenfeld describes it well in his classic book *Is Public School Necessary?* :

> The youngster who passes through its classrooms emerges indoctrinated in a body of secular values as if he had gone to a sort of governmental parochial school. It may not be a very coherent body of values and it may conflict with the values of his parents or religion; but that very incoherence and conflict, combined with a general philosophical confusion, becomes the dominant frame of mind of the graduate. Thus the school building itself seems to have its own spiritual aura, as palpable as that of any church...
>
> *The textbook ... takes the place of the prayer book,* dispensing moral as well as instructional information. This is particularly true in the social sciences, where a secular humanist view of the world is presented virtually as a revealed religion based on unquestioned faith in science and materialism. ***Thus, the rituals of the school replace the rituals of the church*** to fill the youngster's mind with a formalism called "education."[159]

The American school system has become an effective assembly line mass-producing fools and rebels who dare to doubt, deny, and defy the holy Word of God. There was a time when our schools were known for successfully teaching the three "R's," (reading, writing and arithmetic), but now they have, very successfully added a fourth – "rebellion!"

> ***Psalm 14:1,*** *The fool hath said in his heart, there is no God. They are corrupt, they have done abominable works, and there is none that doeth good.*

Sadly, Christians are sending their children by the tens of millions into government-run schools that have become great vehicles of vice and violence. Many, if not most, of these schools are becoming sanctuaries for a sinister and sin-sick sub-culture that is greatly responsible for destroying the moral fiber of this once "great nation."

HIDDEN AGENDAS

Things are not always what they appear to be, especially when it comes to the area of government-run education in America. Thomas Jefferson once said, "Single acts of tyranny may be ascribed to the accidental opinion of the day; but a series of oppressions, begun at a distinguished period, and pursued unalterably through every change of ministry, too plainly prove a deliberate, systematical plan of reducing us to slavery."[160] Is it possible that our educational problems are not really problems at all? Here is a real scorcher from Thomas Sowell, a professor at *Stanford's Hoover Institute*. Dr. Sowell states:

> Virtually everyone has heard how poorly American students are performing, whether compared to foreign students or to American students of a generation ago. What everyone may not know are the specifics of how bad the situation has become, how and *why the public has been deceived*, or the dogmas and *hidden agendas behind it all* ...
>
> The brutal reality is that the American system of education is bankrupt. Allowed to continue as it is, it will absorb ever more vast resources, without any appreciable improvement in the quality of its output, which is already falling behind world standards. Its educational failures cannot be justified, or even mitigated, by its many *non-academic social goals*. It has not merely failed in these areas but has been counterproductive ... This bankruptcy is both in institutions and attitudes.[161]

Is it possible that we have been *deceived by hidden agendas*? Could it be possible that "non-academic social goals" have become a priority in our American schools? Is it possible that, as a nation, and as a church, we have had our proverbial head in the sand and have been reeled in, hook line and sinker, to believe that *it is not as bad as it seems*? Author Dr. Thomas Sowell says:

> *Without the systematic deception of parents* and the public ... it is highly unlikely that the decline in performance could have continued so long. The deeper question that must be asked is why? Whose purposes are being served, and *whose agendas are being advanced*, as American education declines?[162]

The "systematic deception of parents," sounds fairly organized to me. Is it possible that the enemy has ambushed the schools of America, and they are being strategically used for the eventual overthrow of our nation? Let me ask you a probing and perplexing question, "Whose purposes do you think are being served?" I am sure that you would agree with me, probably not the cause of Christ. Listen to this startling statement, made by W.A. John Johnson, an editor for the *Daily News Digest*:

> All America, and especially its parents, have been searching for the answer to the question of what's wrong with our public schools. Bits and pieces of the puzzle have been culled, but no one has been able to put it all together ...

> An *educational mafia captured the high ground of American public education in the late 1800's.* By their own words and deeds...their carefully orchestrated, partially hidden agenda *has deliberately steered the public schools, its teachers and children down a disaster road to socialism, secular humanism*, radicalism, planned failure in reading and writing, suffocation of Christianity, the trashing of basic values...[163]

For the past seventy years these high priests of *secular humanism* and *socialism* have focused their best efforts at transforming the minds of our children and in doing so, they have literally transformed our country. As we informed our readers in *Temples of Darkness*, a major reason for the horrific condition of the public school system today is that it has been permeated with the gradual introduction of *Socialism* and *Secular Humanism*. From a constitutional republic, we have been transformed to a "social democracy," and from our beginnings as a "Christian nation," we are becoming a "secular state."

THE BATTLE IS FOR THE CHILD

"The struggle for the child is a part of the fight for the future of civilization…in the years ahead; we will probably find that the battle has become even fiercer. Organized religion in our nation fully recognizes the difficulties in which it finds itself, and therefore it will increase the efforts in the struggle for the child. For it knows that if it does not, the child may step into a totally secular twenty-first century."[164] ⁻ Atheist, Madelyn Murray O'Hair

From the very beginning, every religious, social and political group has understood the importance of influencing the children of a society if it were to affect (and infect) the society. Our former president, Abraham Lincoln, understood this when he said, "The philosophy of the classroom in this generation will be the philosophy of politics, government and life in the next." Remember our former president, Bill Clinton, also known as "Slick Willie." He was a by-product of the classroom philosophy during the "Swinging Sixties."

Whether the Catholics who declare, "Give us your child for the first seven years, and we will have him for a life-time," or the Communists who have always used education as a form of political indoctrination; a devotion and dedication to the training up of the young has always been first and foremost in the planning of overtaking a civilization. In 1932, William Z.

Foster, then the National Chairman of the Communist Party, U.S.A., wrote in his book *Toward a Soviet America:*

> Among the elementary measures the American Soviet government will adopt to further the cultural revolution are the following: the schools, colleges and universities will be grouped under a National Department of Education and its state and local branches. The studies will be revolutionized, being cleansed of religious, patriotic and other features of bourgeois ideology.[165]

Cleansing the schools of religious and patriotic ideology sounds a bit like what has taken place in our nation over the past forty years. Remember the letter to Owen? Karl Marx, who was an advocate of our style of free and mandatory schooling, wrote in one of the planks of the Communist Manifesto, "free education for all." Marx, like Hitler, Lenin, the Communist Party U.S.A., humanists and many others, have realized the importance of controlling the educational system from top to bottom as a first step to controlling a country.[166]

Another author reminds us, "Those who control what young people are taught and what they experience – what they see, hear, think, and believe will determine the future course for the nation. Given that influence, the predominant value system of an entire culture can be overhauled in one generation, or certainly two, by those with *unlimited access* to the children."[167] Now what organization or institution in America has "unlimited access to the children"? I am sure you would agree, nobody or nothing has more access to the children of our nation like the schools. Would you agree with my humble observation that our value system has been "overhauled?" It's so hard to believe that all of this has taken place under the guise of teaching our children.

These "educrats" understand the importance of changing the values of our children as a pre-requisite to changing the vision of our country. In fact, a special committee to investigate tax-exempt foundations declared in the 83rd Congress, in 1954: "Theoretically a society can be completely made over in something like 15 years, the time it takes to inculcate a new rising crop of youngsters."[168]

It is hard to believe that some of our beloved humanist friends could be as bold as the former Nebraska state Senator, Paul Hoagland, who declared:

> Fundamentalist parents have no right to indoctrinate their children in their beliefs ... *We are preparing their children for the year 2000 and life in a global one-world society* and those children will not fit in.[169]

That's a bit scary, wouldn't you say? If you and I have no right to "indoctrinate" our children, then who has this right? Well, that is where "big brother" comes in. Students enrolled in these government-run and government-controlled *Temples of Darkness* are being indoctrinated daily with teachings that would appall the average parent, if they only knew what was being taught. Thomas Sowell put it this way:

> A variety of courses and programs, under an even wider variety of names, have been set up in schools across the country *to change the values, behavior, and beliefs of American youngsters from what they have been taught by their families* ... this particular door through which such programs enter the school curriculum is far less important than what they do after they have gained entrance.[170]

As one author has informed us, "...The effect of values clarification is to drive a wedge between the parent and child, child and authority and between child and religious beliefs ...

Without exaggeration, it sets up a battle between you and the school for the *very soul of your child*. Considering that the school claims him as a captive audience for five or more hours a day, five days a week, who do you think is winning the battle?" America is at war and some of the most fierce and fatal battles are being fought in the school classrooms. Regrettably, the children of our nation are the causalities!

INDOCTRINATION RATHER THAN INSTRUCTION

In our prior work, we made it clear that most who have done research on the topic, correctly believe that education is no longer really about literacy. The real aim behind much of what takes place on the campuses of our government-run schools today is for the purpose of legitimizing and institutionalizing ungodly policies and practices, which are anti-Christian in nature.

Today the critics of public education are saying things like: "The aim of education is no longer to impart facts and knowledge ... [but] to change the social values of the child away from values that have traditionally been considered fixed, permanent or absolute."[171]

With the eviction of God, by taking prayer and the Bible out of schools in the early 1960's, along with the humanistic teachings of evolution, values clarification, and sex education, our public schools have become 'hot beds' for rearing a generation of 'rebels' who deliberately live in defiance to a holy God and His Word." Listen to atheist and socialist Bertrand Russell who wrote:

> It is expected that advances in psychology will give governments much more control over individual mentality than they now have

> ... *Education should aim at destroying free will,* so that, after pupils have left school, they shall be incapable, throughout the rest of their lives, of thinking or acting otherwise than as their schoolmaster would have wished.[172]

Very interesting thought Mr. Russell. The good old Trojan Horse is being used to destroy the God-given free will of our children. Fancy that! Needless to say, children are extremely impressionable, much like "wet cement." Unlike us "old dogs," they are easy to manipulate and mold into a "new creature." Behavioral scientist, B.F. Skinner, with his "Operant Conditioning," and others like him, understood that "Operant conditioning shapes behavior as a sculptor shapes a lump of clay."[173] It's amazing that they see our children as a lump of clay to be shaped for their ungodly purposes. In his article *"Learning and Teaching in the Future,"* published by the NEA journal *Today's Education* in 1968, John Goodland wrote:

> The most controversial issues of the twenty-first century will pertain to the ends and means of modifying human behavior and who shall determine them. The first educational question will not be "what knowledge is of the most worth?" but *"what kinds of human beings do we wish to produce?"* The possibilities virtually defy our imagination.[174]

Scratching my head, I have to ask, "What kind of human being do they want to produce?" My guess is, probably not a spirit-filled, separated servant of the Lord Jesus Christ. In *Masters of Seduction*, Jeri Lynn Ball writes these thought provoking words:

> Our culture, our tradition, our way of life is being drastically altered right before our very eyes. But these changes are blindly accepted by beguiled Americans, who are deeply enamored of something so subtle, so evil, and so far-reaching that it is tearing apart the moral fabric of this nation and destroying the lives of millions.

What they want is a nation of mindless, cringing, obsequious slaves... With world domination their ultimate goal...they have sought to create a new global social order composed of the dominant elite and their enslaved masses, i.e., men of the herd.

To erect their global structure and communize the world, they have had to build the moral foundation for it: "the new man and new woman" and the "spirit of collectivism." ... [They] do not seek to create just a new way of life, but new human beings. It is not reconstruction of social and cultural institutions that [they] have primarily sought, but reconstruction of human beings.[175]

CHANGE THE VALUES - CHANGE THE VISION

The children in our nation are forced to daily deal with ungodly peer pressure; they are being introduced to a sub-culture of drugs, immorality, and secular humanistic teachings, which contradict all that the child has learned in his Christian home and his church. The minds and souls of our children are being saturated with the garbage of the world at school! It is not uncommon for parents to learn that their children are incapable of reading, writing, or doing basic arithmetic. Far more importantly, they often find that their child has been exposed to sexually graphic material, is being influenced to accept homosexuality as an alternative life-style, and is being taught that the Bible is a myth, and filled with values that are "politically incorrect" and of no real value.

According to the inside flap of Sidney Simons book *Values Clarification: A Handbook of Practical Strategies for Teachers and Students* published in 1972, values clarification makes students aware "of their own ideas, their own beliefs ... their own value systems."[176] Dr. Simon also wrote:

We do not need any more preaching about right and wrong. The old "Thou shalt nots" simply are not relevant. *Values clarification is a method for teachers to change the values of children without getting caught.*[177]

As we shall see, "sex education" has always had an ulterior motive; it never has really been about "safe sex," but more accurately about "breaking down [the child's] inhibitions," which he acquired at home and in the church. Many, including syndicated writer and author Dr. Thomas Sowell, have exposed the "hidden agendas" of government-run education. Sowell writes:

Breaking down inhibitions is the first order of business. That is why so-called "sex education" courses go on for years in some schools. It doesn't take that long to convey the facts of life. But it does take that long to *relentlessly undermine what children have been taught at home.*[178]

Listen to the words from a ninth grade health text: "Testing your ability to function and give pleasure to another person may be less threatening in the early teen years with people of your own sex. *You may come to the conclusion that growing up means rejecting the values of your parents.*"[179] This is a part of the master plan – let's get the children to reject the values of their parents and the principles of God's Word. How can we not recognize that children enrolled in a government-run school system, yea, these *Temples of Darkness*, are being *indoctrinated to a way of life*, and influenced by peers and people whose values are different than our own.

HOMOSEXUALITY

Without a doubt, the most corrupt and cancerous abomination being passed on as education under the godless guise of "tolerance," "respect" and "acceptance" is the horrid homosexual life-style. The homosexuals are using every means possible to desensitize the American people concerning homosexuality. Listen to this quote from an article published in a 1987 *Guide* magazine entitled, *"The Overhauling of Straight America."*

> The first order of business is desensitization of the American public concerning gays and gay rights. To desensitize the public is to help it view homosexuality with indifference instead of with keen emotion.

In just over a decade, the gay movement has achieved this goal. This tolerance, of course, has touched every aspect of our society, including our school systems. The homosexual agenda does not belong in public schools, but many of the nation's public schools have already implemented it in the name of "tolerance," and most of the others are only a step away from implementing these godless, perverted programs. As one writer put it, "The NEA has a captive audience of children and it's planning to use that power to force-feed those children the homosexual agenda." Karen Holgate has made it very clear that the homosexual activists:

> Clearly want all of our children to accept homosexuality as a positive, normal, healthy lifestyle, regardless of what their parents or the Bible or their churches might say. ... They're pitting the school and the state against the values and beliefs of parents.

As we documented in our previous work, many, if not most, schools are being bombarded with literature, videos, and testimonials advocating the pro-gay perspective in public education and the one-sided godless message that students should explore and embrace their homosexual desires.

Concerning the homosexual agenda permeating our government-run schools, O.R. Adams Jr., wrote in *As We Sodomize America,* "The attack on our schools and young people has been insidious and destructive. Another sad aspect of this is that many of our school teachers were parties to the homosexual indoctrination of the children they taught." American schools are becoming a battleground for gay rights activists and gay rights issue. Announces gay activist Donna Redwing, "We're here, we're queer, and we're in the classroom." According to Bob Chase, President of National Education Association, "Schools cannot be neutral when we're dealing with [homosexual] issues, I'm not talking about tolerance. *I'm talking about acceptance.*"

As one author put it, "If parents fully understood what was being taught and what the ramifications were, they would be outraged. There is only one way to accomplish a feat of this magnitude, and that is to isolate kids from their parents and reprogram their values." Listen to A.A. Hodges' concerns of a public educational system, over 150 years ago.

> It is self-evident that on this scheme, if it is consistently and persistently carried out in all parts of the country, the United States system of national popular education will be the most efficient and wide instrument for the propagation of atheism the world has ever seen ... I am as sure as I am of the fact of Christ's reign that a comprehensive and centralized system of national education, separated from religion, as is now commonly proposed, *will prove the most appalling enginery for the propagation of anti-Christian and atheistic unbelief, and of anti-social nihilistic ethics, individual social and political institution which this sin-rent world has ever seen.*[180]

Hodges accurately predicted what would become of a government-controlled system of education that eliminated "religion," and allowed any old special interest group to have their say in how we should educate the children. According to Hodges, the eventual result would be ***the greatest tool of humanism and atheism that our world has ever seen.***

- CHAPTER 6 -

A NATION DIVIDED:
AMERICA'S SECOND CIVIL WAR

"And if a kingdom be divided against itself, that house cannot stand. And if a house be divided against itself, that house cannot stand."

–Mark 3:24-25

Because the shifting sands of secularism have replaced our foundations, the United States of America is not really as united as we would like to think, in spite of the most recent tragedy on September 11, 2001. It must be remembered, " a kingdom (or nation) divided against itself ... cannot stand." In our nation today, we have two rival views of God and man and these views are tearing at the very core of our society. As one author noted, "Civilization based on a Judeo-Christian foundation has collapsed. In its place the West without exception now lives and functions as a pagan world."

The firing on Fort Sumter in April of 1861 ignited the flame of civil war between North and South. Over the next four years of bitter conflict, the struggle for the soul of this nation took went though many tragedies and triumphs, with one side eventually claiming the victory. In his infamous Gettysburg Address, former President Abraham Lincoln declared,

> Now we are engaged in a great civil war, testing whether that nation or any other nation so conceived and so dedicated, can long endure. We are met on a great battlefield of that war. ... It is for us the living, rather to be dedicated here to the unfinished work

111

which they have fought ... It is rather for us to be here dedicated to the great task remaining before us - that from these honored dead we take increased devotion to the cause for which they gave the last full measure of devotion – that we highly resolve that these dead have not died in vain – that this nation, under God, shall have a new birth of freedom – and that the government of the people, shall not perish from the earth.[181]

Lincoln's words still ring true today. We, in America, "are engaged in a great civil war," but this is not a war fought with bullets and bombs, but rather a war that is being waged over ideas, philosophies, and principles. This battle that is raging is "testing whether [this] nation ... can long endure." But not just simply enduring as a nation, but as the nation which was "conceived in liberty," a nation which was founded and flourished for over 200 years as a republic that was birthed as "One Nation Under God."

As Lincoln called for Americans to commit themselves to "the unfinished work" and to be "dedicated to the great task" which remained before them, we too, must devote ourselves to reclaim America for God and for good. If we do not do so, "the government of the people, shall ... perish from the earth."

Although Abraham Lincoln would no doubt be staggered at the current political, economic, and spiritual condition of the nation that he led through its darkest hour, he appears to have had remarkable flashes of insight into what possibly lay ahead. In an 1837 speech, while recognizing the virtual invulnerability of the United States, he then asked a very pertinent question:

At what point then is the approach of danger to be expected? I answer, if it comes, it must spring up among us, and it cannot come from abroad. If destruction be our lot, we must ourselves be its author and finisher. As a nation of freemen, we must live through all time or die of suicide.

Lincoln's observation, "If destruction be our lot, we must ourselves be its author and finisher." Suicide – now that is an interesting thought. On the other hand, could it be homicide? Has our nation committed suicide or has our constitutional republic been murdered? Is it possible that a country as big and powerful as the United States of America could be overtaken, and without much of a struggle? Surely most Americans would have the sense to recognize if sinister forces were at work deliberately and deceptively destroying our once great constitutional republic.

In the same way the people of God shared a country, but not a culture with the Egyptians and the Babylonians. We in America now share a country, but not a culture with a great host of people who have accepted the secular humanistic philosophies of the day. Our nation is divided straight down the middle. "Our divisions are rooted in our deepest beliefs," writes Pat Buchanan, "and upon those beliefs Americans are almost as divided as we were when General Beauregard gave the order to fire on Fort Sumter. Once again, we are seceding from one another; only this time, it is the secession of the heart."[182]

We are no longer the same America. After the 2000 election, pollster William McInturf told the *Washington Post*: "We have two massive colliding forces. One is ... Christian, religiously conservative." The other, writes McInturff, "is socially tolerant, pro-choice, [and] secular ..."[183]

Our primary differences in America are not economic; they are ethical. Our divide in America isn't based upon money, but on morals. We are in the midst of a great conflict in the battle of ideology. We are in the midst of a battle of worldviews. The conflict is between those who hold true to the traditional, Judeo-Christian biblical value system, and those who would hold true to a secular, humanistic worldview. The two contrasting views are locked in deadly combat in a winner-take-all battle.

President Bush, in his inaugural address, was right when he said, "And sometimes our differences run so deep, it seems we share a continent, but not a country."[184]

It shouldn't be hard to distinguish; we have become two nations, two peoples with our varied differences becoming more profound with each passing day. As one author has written, "An older America is passing away, and a New America is coming into its own …"[185]

CONFLICTING CONVICTIONS

We are living in the midst of a very great conflict, one that has been brewing for quite some time. This conflict is indeed a combat zone of personal and public convictions. Moreover, the real issue at hand is simply this – Is the Word and will of God relevant for everyday life here in America in the year 2002?

Thus when we hear the rhetoric about "One Nation Under God," – don't believe it for a moment! It just simply isn't true, and if we don't understand the reality and ramifications of the conflict, we lose the war by default and lose the country to a secular humanistic and paganistic culture. In his book, *America's Real War*, Rabbi and author Daniel Lapin states:

> Dividing Americans along these two fault lines begins to make sense of what has actually been taking place in our nation over the past forty to fifty years. Only when we become conscious of these two diametrically divergent nations struggling to gain dominance in America will the lawless landscape surrounding us begin to make sense. As a nation and as a people, we are taking into consideration whether God and biblical morality should be allowed to reign supreme in our land or should they be kept within the confines of the church house. The debate isn't scientific, it isn't social, but the debate that is overwhelming our country is a spiritual debate.

THE "AT-RISK" GENERATION

There is a great chasm in our land. Our understanding of what is taking place and our recognition of the "enemies within our borders" is essential. This generation in which we live can and should be referred to as the "At-Risk" generation. Why, you ask? The answer, naturally, is because we are "At-Risk" of losing our children, our traditional American culture and our country to the secular "sleepers" in America.

In his most recent book, *The Death of the West*, Patrick Buchanan writes, "For the first time since Andrew Jackson drove the British out of Louisiana in 1815, a foreign enemy is inside the gates, and the American people are at risk in their own country."[186] Unfortunately, our enemies are within the confines of our borders, and they appear to be winning the war. Because of their concerted efforts and our often complacent spirit, "They have replaced the good country we grew up in with a cultural wasteland and a moral sewer that are not worth living in and not worth fighting for," and for the most part, it has become "their country not ours."[187]

Regrettably, most Bible believers have not come to recognize the conflict that is raging in our public schools, public-square and in our political arena. So many people who share traditionalist views appear not to know a war is going on – a conflict that will have profound implications for future generations. Our adversaries have a specific agenda in mind for the future of our children, for our country, and for human civilization.

It is hard for us to conceive that for years now, men in high places have had in the back of their mind a hidden agenda – an agenda to deceive and destroy not only the God-given freedoms our forefathers intended for us to enjoy, but also that which God's Word has afforded us.

CORRUPTED CULTURE

"Culture," argues Robert Bork, in his book *Slouching Towards Gomorrah*, "refers to all human behavior and institutions, including popular entertainment, art, religion, education, scholarship, economic activity, science, technology, law, and morality." He continues with this revealing statement, "Of that list, only science, technology, and the economy may be said to be healthy today, and it is problematical how long that will last."[188] He is accurate stating, "Not a single American institution, from popular music to higher education to science, has remained untouched."[189] In his book, Bork makes a profound observation, saying:

> [T] here is currently a widespread sense that the distinctive virtues of American life, indeed the distinctive features of Western civilization, are in peril in ways not previously seen. This time the threat is not military ... nor is it external. This time we face, and seem to be succumbing to, an attack mounted by a force not only within Western civilization but one that is perhaps its legitimate child.[190]

Perverted philosophical ideas are attacking the authority of the family, the church and the value system envisioned by our founders. Our enemies are *redefining* and *restructuring* every aspect of our society in such a way that it fits into a politically correct "mold" for a society that wants nothing to do with God and His Word.

> **Psalm 14:1,** *"The fool hath said in his heart, there is no God. They are corrupt, they have done abominable works, there is none that doeth good."*

Radical revolutionists have undermined the value system that made this nation both glorious and great. The revolution, for the most part, has been a revolution of ideas and ideology. "But where Lenin's revolution failed," writes Buchanan, "the one that erupted on the campuses in the sixties succeeded. It put down roots in society, and it created a new America."[191] A century ago, Gustavo Le Bon wrote in his classic *The Crowd*:

> The real cause of the great upheavals which precede changes of civilizations, such as the fall of the Roman Empire and the rise of the Arabian Empire, is a profound modification in the ideas of the peoples ... *The memorable events of history are the visible effects of the invisible changes of human thought* ...[192]

As we well know, what we believe as a nation determines how we will behave as a nation. Therefore, the subtle undercurrents of despicable and demonic philosophies that have crept into the American thought process is tearing at the moral seams of the nation.

> *Proverbs 23:7, "For as he thinketh in his heart, so is he..."*
>
> *2 Corinthians 10:3-5, "For though we walk in the flesh, we do not war after the flesh: (For the weapons of our warfare are not carnal, but mighty through God to the pulling down strongholds;) Casting down imaginations, and every high thing that exalteth itself against the knowledge of God, and bringing into captivity every thought to the obedience of Christ."*
>
> *Colossians 2:8, "Beware lest any man spoil you through philosophy and vain deceit, after the tradition of men, after the rudiments of the world, and not after Christ."*

Our adversaries have permeated and polluted America with "socialistic," "humanistic," and "atheistic" worldviews – eliminating both God and the family from the picture. These philosophies are "not after Christ," but after the spirit of anti-Christ. They have divided our nation in two. Basically, I would agree with author Daniel Lapin who says, "People are now lining up with each other according to how they answer two essential questions:

Do you yearn for an America in which God is allowed and honored outside of our churches and synagogues, or do you want an America in which lip service is paid to Him so long as He is kept out of the real world?

Do you accept a view of God that would be compatible with one that your religion held 223 years ago at the founding of this country, or have you reinvented God to fit in with your present-day view?[193]

I am of the same opinion with Dr. Phil Stringer who declared, "As the foundation of our Christian culture has faded, so has our respect for human life (which is based upon the self-evident truth of creation). As our historic Christian culture has been swept away, so has our liberty (to be replaced with dependence upon big government). A culture war rages in the United States to determine whether the last vestiges of our Christian culture will be swept away, or whether there will be a return to our foundations."[194]

In spite of all of our beautiful buildings, expanded numbers and varied programs, "By the twenty-first century, the de-Christianization of our public life was complete."[195] The dumbing down of our schools, the de-valuing of our nation and the "dethronement of God from public life was not done democratically, it was done dictatorially, and our forefathers would never have tolerated it."[196] As Buchanan wrote:

With the de-Christianization of America has come the overthrow of the old moral order based on Judeo-Christian teachings and the establishment of the new moral order of the Humanist Manifesto. Again, this was not done by popular vote, but by court order.

Abortion had been a crime; now it is right. So saith the Court. Voluntary school prayer now violates the First Amendment, but nude nightclub dancing no longer does. When Colorado voted in a referendum to stop the legalization of homosexuality, the

Supreme Court decided that the motives of the voters were suspect and threw it out.[197]

As one author declared, "Politics is a major part of this battlefield." However, it isn't the most important one. We must not make the same mistake many of our adversaries have made by "identifying politics as the heart of the battle." No, this battle is being waged on many fronts. Just to name a few of the most notable: Church, State, education, art, economics, and all the areas of life that are engulfed in sin and in need of revival and reform. Politics is just one of many different aspects in the battle for pre-eminence in our country. Concerning political action, I have to agree with author Gary North who said:

> The battle for political dominion will not be won primarily through political action. Politics is the working out of religious first principles in the civil realm. It is a battle over the true nature of God, man, law, and time.[198]

CUTTING THE TIE THAT BINDS

"How long halt ye between two opinions?" - 1 Kings 18:21

Christians must come to grip with a very important biblical principle, "No fence straddling allowed!" For far too long, we have been straddling the fence and "halting" between two opinions. Many Bible teachers inform us that we are living in the Laodicean age. I would have to agree with them. A lukewarm spirit has engulfed the church of Jesus Christ. We have become comfortable, complacent and show very little concern for reaching our world with the gospel of Jesus Christ. Materialism and hedonism appear to be the "virtues of the hour.

119

Revelation 3:15-16, I know thy works, that thou art neither cold nor hot: I would that thou wert cold or hot. So then because thou art lukewarm, and neither cold nor hot, I will spue thee out of My mouth.

The cultural divide that we see in our nation is also very evident in our churches. As a church we are enjoying our "prosperity," and doing everything we can to avoid persecution. It is high time that we make a choice between secularism and a Scriptural life-style.

Joshua 24:15, "And if it seem evil unto you to serve the Lord, choose you this day whom ye will serve ..."

One author put it well saying, "When they are divorced from everyday living, the two competitors, secularism and Judeo-Christian religion, seem to do well, co-existing side by side in the community, the university, and even in the same persons mind and heart. But when the rudimentary principles of these two belief systems are applied to critical issues of family and society, of life and death, they clash." "The goal," writes Pat Buchanan, "of the secularists is to cut the ties between our culture and "common religion." If that happens, the culture dies.[199] Dr. Russell Kirk made it clear:

All culture arises out of religion. When religious faith decays, culture must decline, though often seeming to flourish for a space after the religion, which has nourished it, has sunk into disbelief. But neither can religion subsist if severed from a healthy culture.[200]

CONSERVATIVE OR COUNTERREVOLUTIONARY

"Ye are the salt of the earth: but if the salt have lost his savor, wherewith shall it be salted? It is thenceforth good for nothing, but to be cast out, and to be trodden under the foot of men. Ye are the light of the world. A city that is set on a hill cannot be hid. Let your light so shine before men,

that they may see your good works, and glorify your father which is in heaven." – Matthew 5:13-14 & 16

The people of God are to be the preserving agent in this decaying world. We are to be a light in the midst of darkness, a reflection of the light and glory of Jesus Christ. Because we have not allowed our "light to shine," and because our salt has lost its savor, this nation has become rotten to the core, changing dramatically into a very unhealthy culture – a culture that not only rejects the Christian value system, but also has become antagonistic to the Word and ways of God. T. S. Eliot wrote:

> If Christianity goes, the whole of culture goes. Then you must start painfully again, and you cannot put on a new culture ready-made… You must pass through many centuries of barbarism. We should not live to see the new culture, nor would our great-great-grand children; and if we did not one of us would be happy in it.[201]

Those of us who truly love our country and the culture which made this country great must come to grips with this question: Are we to simply and passively conserve the remnant, or are we willing to fight and take the culture back? As Pat Buchanan asks, "Are we conservatives, or must we also become counterrevolutionaries and overthrow the dominant culture?"[202]

Our days and desire to stand and be counted as a "conservative" have come to a swift and sure end. It is time to become a counterrevolutionary who is willing to fight and overturn what has crept into our culture. Concerning our unwillingness to stand up and fight, Buchanan is right when he states:

> Traditionalists can run, but they can't hide. With our public schools and Public Square de-Christianized, our private schools and private institutions are next. Through the hook of public money, all will be made godless, all forced to conform to the

catechism of the revolution that declares infallibly, "All lifestyles are equal."[203]

Sad to say, but the fundamental "religious right," once known as the "Moral Majority," has been transformed into the silent majority. Buchanan calls them the Intimidated Majority. In his book *The Death of the West*, in a chapter entitled "Intimidated Majority," Buchanan asks the stinging question, "Why did Christians permit their God and faith to be driven out of the temples of their civilization? Why was their resistance so low?" In his book *Long March*, Roger Kimball, an editor at New Criterion, attributes the rout on the cultural front to a failed conservative movement. He writes:

> The long march of America's cultural revolution has succeeded beyond the wildest dreams of all but the most starry-eyed utopians. The great irony is that the victory took place in the midst of a significant drift to the center-right in electoral politics.
>
> The startling and depressing fact is that supposed conservative victories at the polls have done almost nothing to challenge the dominance of left wing, emancipationist attitudes and ideas in our culture. On the contrary, in the so-called "culture wars," conservatives have been conspicuous losers.[204]

THE GREAT CONSERVATIVE SELL-OUT

Contrary to what the establishment "conservatives" would have us to believe, "the 80's and 90's have become the final boost to the European levels of socialism in the United States." As one author reminds us, "We are taxed to fund educational, cultural, and philosophical programs that we despise."[205] For example:

    ❑ The Federal Government distributed 849,000 condoms in 1992.

❑ Our tax money is directed to kill babies in their mother's womb. Federal spending on family planning surged from $375,000,000 to $483,000,000 in the four-year reign of King George (Bush, Sr.). This funding has increased from $70 million in 1981.

❑ According to Howard Phillips, 122 pro-sodomy organizations are propped up by federal funding – grants that average $200,000 each.

❑ The United States federal government spends $15,450 annually on each AIDS patient – in comparison to $285 for cancer patients, $33 for heart and vascular disease patients, and $25 for diabetes patients.[206]

George Grant, author of *Grand Illusions,* informs us: "Today government funding provides the majority of revenues at more than half of Planned Parenthood affiliates. Nineteen different federal appropriations measures pour millions of dollars into its cankered coffers every year through dozens of agencies, programs and projects." In his book, Grant makes the point that *our tax money* is used to promote abortion, pay for buildings where abortions are performed, and fund programs that encourage people to kill their babies.[207]

Twentieth century Christians have tried to work with the Republican Party, achieving the election of Ronald Reagan in 1980 and 1984. Reagan "promised to appoint pro-life justices and reduce government regulations." Instead, writes one author, "We received Sandra Day O'Connor, more government programs, more funding to the pro-abortion Planned Parenthood organizations, and exponential Federal Government expansion through government spending." The author continues by writing:

> The Christians turned to endorse the Republican, George Bush, who proposed budgets that funded homosexual art, grants to prostitutes, increased funds for Planned Parenthood, and we received the first abortionist to ever serve on the Supreme Court –

David Souter. Taxes went up, unlawful search and seizures burgeoned, Federal Government regulations and spending grew exponentially, and not many could vote for Mr. Bush in 1992 with a clear conscience. Twentieth century American Christians have become supremely unsuccessful in the political realm.[208]

WE HAVE TO BE WILLING TO FIGHT

"The first thing we have to learn about fighting and winning a culture war," said Dr. Sam Francis, the syndicated columnist and author of *Revolution from the Middle* "is that we are not fighting to 'conserve' something, we are fighting to overthrow something."[209] Francis claims:

> We must understand clearly and firmly that the dominant authorities in ... the major foundations, the media, the schools, the universities, and most of the system of organized culture, including the arts and entertainment–not only do nothing to conserve what most of us regard as our traditional way of life, but actually seek its destruction or are indifferent to its survival. If our culture is going to be conserved, then we need to dethrone the dominant authorities that threaten it.[210]

In our nation, this conflict is raging. This conflict has always existed, but in recent decades the differences of values and vision between the two opponents has become clearer and more distinct. Without a doubt, we have reached a stage in our history where darkness and light are in a great spiritual conflict for space. If we are not willing to stand up for Christ in our culture, we lose the war by default. Someone or something will prevail. Who or what will prevail? We have reached a point in time, much as our ancestors did just before the Civil War. The Civil War was the most tragic and heroic time in the history of our nation. Lapin reminds us:

> When the Civil War was fought, the individuals participating were not enemies. Often, they were neighbors and cousins; in

> more than one instance they were brothers. On both sides fought upright, valiant soldiers. However, they had reached a point where their conflicting beliefs could no longer coexist in one country. A terrible war ensued, but at the end of the fighting, one idea again prevailed. Once again, we were one country, "This time the culture war, thankfully, is not a bloody one. That makes it no less a war that will, in the end, yield a victor and a loser. The two ideas struggling for supremacy in society today cannot coexist. One needs to dominate.[211]

Unfortunately, everyone loses when the culture is brought down, including our capitalistic economic system which will "be replaced with one or another variety of statism presiding over a degenerate society,"[212] writes Bork. We may have won the Cold War, but we are definitely losing the Culture War. The foundations of this great Republic have been diminished with very little hope of being restored to their rightful place.

The day and age in which we live has been called, by many the "Post-Christian Age" – or the "Age of Unbelief," an age in which there are no absolutes, a day in which "every man does that which is right in his own eyes." As Dr. Henry Morris has noted, the Post-Christian Age, is a time "when almost any kind of belief and practice except biblical Christianity is tolerated and even encouraged."[213] Of course, it has not always been this way in America–times have changed, dramatically!

Far from our roots as a Christian nation, we now find ourselves "on the slippery slope of unbelief," with generations of people having had their own faith shipwrecked by "the spurious theories of scholars" who have attacked the Word of God in every conceivable fashion and have literally annihilated the value system of our nation. Men like Charles Darwin, Karl Marx, Wilhelm Wundt, Nietzsche, Thomas Huxley, Harry Emerson Fosdick, John Dewey, B.F. Skinner, Alfred Kinsey and a host of others have been responsible for delivering the messages and designing the methods that have destroyed this once great nation.

"It is clear," writes author David Noebel in his book *The Battle for Truth*, "that the agenda of the Secular Humanists is exerting a much greater impact on our culture than traditional orthodox Christianity." He continues with this indicting statement:

> The Christian worldview has been, to a large degree, deliberately eradicated from the public square. The Secular Humanists have cleverly and methodically gained ascendancy over Christianity in the past two to three generations with an attack that has been concentrated and deliberate. Christian ideas and ideals have been under siege in all areas.[214]

Yes, there is a great division in our land today. Decadence is the virtue of the hour. Darkness seems to be darker today than ever before. But the good news is that the light of Christ reflecting off of His people can overcome the darkness.

Isaiah 60:1-3, "*Arise, shine; for thy light is come, and the glory of the Lord is risen upon thee. For, behold, the darkness shall cover the earth, and gross darkness the people: but the Lord shall arise upon thee. And the Gentiles shall come to thy light, and kings to the brightness of thy rising.*"

"Not until I went to the churches of America and heard her pulpits aflame with righteousness did I understand the secret of her genius and power. America is great because she is good ... and if America ceases to be good, America will cease to be great."

-ALEXIS DE TOCQUEVILLE

- CHAPTER 7 -

CEASING TO BE GOOD

"The wicked shall be turned into hell,

and all the nations that forget God."

- Psalm 9:17

As a nation, we had a glorious beginning, but we have strayed from our roots. We are definitely not the same nation that once was the envy of the world. It seems that helplessness and hopelessness are abounding in our once proud and prosperous nation. The sinister seeds sown during the "Swinging Sixties," the do-your-own-thing era, "germinated over the next quarter century, bearing a bumper crop of poisonous fruit."[215] The wickedness that abounds in our nation will, in due time, bring her down. To paraphrase one author, "I have seen the future, and it's given me a massive migraine."

During the nineteenth century, France's Alexis de Tocqueville came to America in an attempt to find what it was that made America such a great and glorious nation. He wrote in *Democracy in America*, "I sought for the greatness and genius of America in her commodious harbors and her ample rivers ... and it was not there; in her fertile lands and boundless prairies ... and it was not there."[216] He traveled far and near seeking to find what made us great; he did not find our greatness in our natural resources. It was found, he said, when:

> I went to the churches of America and heard *her pulpits aflame with righteousness* did I understand the secret of her genius and

129

power. America is great because she is good ... and *if America ceases to be good, America will cease to be great.*[217]

Notice those words, "pulpits aflame with righteousness." That is where the greatness of America found its source. By the way, we still need "pulpits that are aflame with righteousness." America needs men who are called by God, consecrated unto God, and committed to the service of God. America needs men who are willing to "Cry aloud, spare not, lift up thy voice like a trumpet, and shew My people their transgression" (Isaiah 58:1). John Adams, our second president once said,

> It is the duty of the clergy to accommodate their discourses to the times, to preach against such sins as are most prevalent and to recommend such virtues as are most wanted.

Unfortunately, we live in a day in which "silence is golden," especially in reference to speaking out against the "besetting" sins of America in the twenty-first century. De Tocqueville also warned us "if America ceases to be good, America will cease to be great." He clearly understood what our present day leaders in America don't – that *America's greatness is dependent upon America's goodness*!

The greatness of our nation can never be separated from the goodness of our nation. Even before de Tocqueville came to the shores of our country, Thomas Jefferson understood this to be true. Jefferson stated, "Can the liberties of a nation be thought secure when we have removed their only firm basis, a conviction in the minds of the people that these liberties are the gift from God."

Though our nation was at one time, rightly referred to as a Christian nation, this is no longer the case. America is now a pluralistic and pagan nation. As one author noted, "A nation will have one God or many. Ours is increasingly polytheistic."[218] This same author rightly notes:

> The gods of the twentieth century America include the doctrines of radical autonomy, of absolute rights divorced from responsibilities, of gender sameness, of self-expression, (which acknowledges no higher purpose), of moral relativism and sexual indulgence. Their temples are courtrooms, legislative chambers, classrooms, newsrooms, and the executive suites of entertainment conglomerates and publishing firms. We are one nation under God no more.[219]

Thanks to our indifference and our opponents' insistence, this is no longer a Christian nation. In the words of Jewish Conservative, Don Feder:

> By *Pagan America* I mean that this is no longer a Judeo-Christian nation, animated by the ethical vision of the Bible, with its special emphasis on honesty, hard work, caring, and self-discipline. Instead, we are evolving into the type of Canaanite culture (unrestrained hedonism, ritual prostitution, child sacrifice and the civic virtue of Sodom), which my ancestors encountered at the dawn of moral history.[220]

LEAVE OUR MORAL ROOTS, LOSE OUR FREEDOM

"When the righteous are in authority the people rejoice." - Proverbs 29:2

All one has to do is study the moral decline in the 1770's France, 1910's Russia, and 1930's Germany to recognize moral decline precedes tyranny. One author said it this way, "You will find the precedent to tyranny is a rise in homosexuality, fornication, adultery, abortion, infanticide, and pornography."[221] Both political and religious freedom is only viable and attainable under the influence of a "righteous" people

We have forgotten God, and because of this, our nation is quickly becoming a nation of infidels and idolaters. The born-again patriot, Patrick Henry, also reminds us what happens when a nation forgets God. Henry said:

> Bad men cannot make good citizens. It is impossible that a nation of infidels or idolaters should be a nation of free men. It is when a people forget God that tyrants forge their chains.[222]

The Quaker, and founder of Pennsylvania, William Penn, understood the inevitable result of a nation that forgets God. He said that, "If we will not be governed by God, we will be ruled by tyrants."[223]

Over the past 100 years, Christians have been lured into a state of slumber, security and have been seduced into believing in "ethical neutrality." Our adversaries (and there are many) want us to see "the cultural and governmental realm as a neutral field." Of course, in all reality, there is no neutrality – someone's value system will be the controlling system of the day. Machiavelli's dream of a complete secular state is becoming a reality right under our noses. Swanson, in his book *The Last Mayflower,* states:

> As Christians relaxed the application of Biblical truth in society, education, culture, and family, the ungodly rushed in quietly to fill the void. As the homosexuals, the humanists, and the socialists gain the political upper hand, they then will crush the Christians who slowly awaken from their stupor of pretended neutrality.... This is a historical lesson that should be learned well by this generation. Never let up in this war between good and evil. It will be God's law or man's law.[224]

In his book, *The Death of the West*, Pat Buchanan warns us:

> America has just undergone a cultural revolution, with a new elite now occupying the commanding heights. Through its capture of

the institutions that shape and transmit ideas, opinions, beliefs, and values–TV, the arts, entertainment, education, - this elite is creating a new people. Not only ethnically and racially, but also culturally and morally, we are no longer one people or "one nation under God."

Millions have begun to feel like strangers in their own land. They recoil from a popular culture that is saturated with raw sex and trumpets hedonistic values. They see old holidays disappear and old heroes degraded. They see the art and artifacts of a glorious past removed from their museums and replaced by depressing, the ugly, the abstract, and the anti-American. They watch as books they cherished disappear from the schools they attended, to be replaced by authors they have never heard of. The moral code that they were raised to live by has been overthrown. The culture they grew up with is dying inside the country they grew up in.

In half a lifetime, many Americans have seen their God dethroned, their heroes defiled, their culture polluted, their values assaulted, their country invaded, and themselves demonized as extremists and bigots for holding on to beliefs Americans held for generations.[225]

The renown Edmund Burke once said, "To make us love our country, our country ought to be lovely."[226] In far too many ways, as Pat Buchanan said,

America is no longer lovely. Though she remains a great country, many wonder if she is still a good country. Our world has been turned upside down. What was right and true yesterday is wrong and false today. What was immoral and shameful–promiscuity, abortion, euthanasia, suicide–has become praiseworthy. Nietzsche called it the transvaluation of all values; the old virtues become sins, and the old sins become virtues.[227]

Unfortunately, over the past four decades the political and religious left made up of communists, socialists, humanists, feminists, new-agers and a multitude of others have dominated the educational, entertainment and political systems of our nation. The subverting of the once so great American spirit, which has been taking place over the last forty to fifty years, has diluted all the basic fundamentals upon which once made this nation great and has turned it into a sin-sick society.

In the wealthiest, mightiest, most liberated and most tolerant nation on earth, "the impoverishment of the spirit has led to a values depression."[228] Author Des Griffin was right when he said of America's new image:

> The new image is one of a lumbering, stumbling, bumbling, grumbling dolt who staggers from one crisis to another through a blinding haze of fear and indecision ... It is the image of a terribly sick giant who, having exchanged his God-given heritage for a bowl of humanistic Socialist pottage, has lost his sense of destiny and purged his mind of any trace of morality–a rebel whose reasoning processes are so devious, so scrambled as to be beyond comprehension.[229]

THE FALL OF THE ROMAN EMPIRE

"Rome, there is nothing like thee, although thou art almost wholly ruined."
– A Latin Poet

Historian Will Durant once noted, "The two greatest problems in history [are] how to account for the rise of Rome, and how to account for her fall."[230] Accounting for Rome's fall isn't really as difficult as Mr. Durant would have us to believe. As author Austin Sorenson has stated, "Rome forgot the glory of her destiny,"[231] and because of it, she slid into historical oblivion. Many authors have compared Rome's rise and fall with our own present predicament. In *The Greek and Roman World*, W.G. Hardy wrote:

> The world of the Roman Empire in the first two centuries is almost frighteningly similar to modern North America in its

excesses and in its wealth and, above all, in its devotion to materialistic success at the expense of the spiritual and the intellectual.[232]

As we have already mentioned, countries that lose their historical focus will eventually lose their will to live – so it was for Rome and so it is for America. Immorality is always the by-product of Scriptural ignorance and indifference. When a nation loses sight of its divine purpose, it will lose its purity and principle. As one historian remarked, Rome "had decayed within before it was overthrown from without."[233]

As many have noted, "The average age of the world's civilizations has been 200 years."[234] Quite a few authors have informed us of the cycle that Rome went through and what other nations who have died have gone through. They went:

- ❏ From bondage to spiritual faith
- ❏ From spiritual faith to great courage
- ❏ From courage to liberty
- ❏ From liberty to abundance
- ❏ From abundance to selfishness
- ❏ From selfishness to complacency
- ❏ From complacency to dependence
- ❏ From dependence back again to bondage

America is 226 years old. Where do you think she is in the above cycle? In his book *The Decline and Fall of the Roman Empire*, written in 1788, Edward Gibbon has noted five reasons why great civilizations die:

- ❏ The undermining of the dignity and sanctity of the home, which is the basis for human society

135

❑ Higher and higher taxes and the spending of public money for free bread circuses for the populaces

❑ The mad craze for pleasure – sports becoming every year more exciting, more brutal, more immoral

❑ The building of great armaments when the real enemy is within – the decay of individual responsibility

❑ The decay of religion – with faith fading into a mere form, losing touch with real life, losing power to guide people[235]

Sound familiar? It should! Many outstanding authors have warned us that the demise of the Roman Empire "was brought about by the same national diseases that are presently wracking the United States and other nations in the West."[236] What are these "diseases" that are debilitating our nation? A few of the many are rampant crime, inflation, breakup of the home, immorality, abortion, homosexuality, a great increase in government bureaucracy, welfarism, the decline of patriotism and the collapse of the national resolve.

Concerning childrearing, Jerome Carcopino wrote, "Having given up the habit of controlling their children, they let their children govern them, and took pleasure bleeding themselves white to gratify the expensive whims of their offspring."[237] The result according to Carcopino was that "they were succeeded by a generation of idlers and wasters, who had grown accustomed to luxury and lost all sense of discipline."[238]

Isaiah 3:1-5, "For, behold, the Lord of hosts, doth take away from Jerusalem and from Judah the ... The mighty man, and the man of war, the judge, and the prophet, and the prudent, and the ancient, And I will give children to be their princes, and babes shall rule over them. And the people shall be oppressed every one by another, and every one by his neighbor: the child shall behave himself proudly against the ancient ... "

This same Carcopino informs us that a strong "women's rights" movement developed in Roman society. He continues, "Some [wives] evaded the duties of maternity for fear of losing their good looks, some took pride in being behind their husbands in no sphere of activity, and vied with them the tests of strength which their sex would seem to forbid; some were not content to live their lives by their husband's side, but carried on another life without him ... it is obvious that unhappy marriages must have been innumerable."[239]

Caropino notes that schools in the great Roman Empire, "undermined instead of strengthened the children's morals, they mishandled the children's bodies instead of developing them."[240] Like the children of our nation, Roman children received an education with no set value system, and no sense of nation pride. Author Phillip Myers states:

> The Roman virtues – honesty, candor, frugality and patriotism – withered and died. What was left was a people whom neither the vices of the rulers nor the increasingly bold attacks of foreign enemies could shake out of their apathy.[241]

Concerning Rome's entertainment, Myers writes, "The Roman stage was *gross* and *immoral*. It was one of the main agencies to which must be attributed the undermining of the originally sound moral life of Roman society. So absorbed did the people become in the indecent representations on the stage, that they lost all thought and cares for the affairs of real life."[242] Blatant hedonism and paganism overran the Roman Empire. The Romans, according to Carpocino:

> reveled in the thrills and excitement of sport spectaculars. They were caught up in a 'feverish rush for excitement,' for something new to feed the sated senses. They "thrilled with barbaric joy" and "could not restrain their delight" at the sight of the bloodiest conflicts. The thousands of Romans who, day after day, from

137

morning till night, could take pleasure in this slaughter and not spare a tear for those whose sacrifice multiplied their [gambling] stakes, were learning nothing but contempt for human life and dignity.[243]

Francis Schaeffer lists a few Roman distinctives that are worth noting: "… A mounting love of show and luxury (that is, affluence); second, a widening gap between the very rich and the very poor; third, an obsession with sex; fourth, freakishness in the arts… fifth, an increased desire to live off the state.[244]

Rome of yesteryear, sounds a bit like the United States of America today. Santayanas' quote: "Those who don't know history are doomed to repeat it," would seem to be very appropriate for us to take to heart. The words of another might help us to "wake up" and recognize the season we presently find ourselves in. "The highways of history are strewn with the wreckage of the nations that forgot God."

THE HOME

According to our recent *Census 2000*, the results of forgetting God and "sowing to the flesh" over the past fifty years have brought home quite a harvest. The results are disappointing, disgusting and discouraging. If we do not wake up soon and recognize what is happening around us and do something about it while we can, we will be in trouble. A few of the surprises the *Census 2000* revealed are that:

- ❏ Households headed by unmarried partners (most of them involving people living together out of wedlock) grew by almost 72 percent during the past decade.

- ❏ Households headed by single mothers or fathers increased by 25 percent and 62 percent, respectively, and for the first time ever, nuclear families dropped below 25 percent of the households.

❏ Thirty-three percent of all babies born were born to unmarried women, compared to only 3.8 percent in 1940.

❏ Other studies show that cohabitation increased by nearly 1,000 percent between 1962 and 1998, and that households headed by the homosexual couples are soaring.[245]

The cultural tsunami known as the sexual revolution, which overwhelmed our nation during the "Swinging Sixties," has left the traditional family and traditional family values, as found in the Scriptures, in disarray. The number of couples "shacking up" jumped nearly ten-fold between 1960 and 1998, while married couples plummeted from almost three-quarters of all households to just over half.[246] Not surprisingly, illegitimacy has skyrocketed 511 percent in the past forty years.[247]

These and other statistics like them reveal that the old ship *glory* is sinking, and she is sinking fast. We see that the God-ordained institution of the family is disintegrating at a more rapid pace than ever in the history of our nation. We see ungodly taboos of just a generation ago becoming the trends of our day. Our society is perishing because we have exchanged the truth of God's Word for the lies of the world around us. There is no doubt that our nation has fallen on hard times.

Hosea 8:7, *For they have sown the wind, and they shall reap the whirlwind.*

There has been an increase in violence, vulgarity and vice. Almost 16 million children have witnessed a violent crime, including robbery, stabbing, shooting, murder, or domestic abuse. One out of eight people murdered in our nation are under 18.

Sixty-one percent of TV shows depicted violent acts in 1997 compared with 58 percent in 1995. TV viewers watch an average of six acts of violence per hour (excluding verbal abuse or violence precipitated by natural disasters). Between 1995 and 1997, there was a 47 percent jump in vulgarity used on TV during the family hour. Disney-owned ABC led the networks with 3.47 sexual references. Other networks averaged 1.67; GLAAD (The Gay & Lesbian Alliance Against Defamation) has happily noted that the 1997 TV network lineup included a record setting 30 lesbian, gay, and bisexual characters, a 23 percent increase over the 1996 line up.[248]

TELEVISION

Since we are on the topic of television, let us take just a moment to bring out a few interesting tidbits. Don Wildmon reports that 88 percent of sexual activity in prime-time television is between people who are not married.[249] Many of the daily talk shows seem to exalt sexual perversion. For example, one of the guests on a recent **daytime** talk show was a woman who claimed to have had sex with 250 men in a span of ten hours.[250]

As Hollywood actor Woody Allen once said, "The reason Beverly Hills is so clean is because they turn their garbage into television programs!" Sad, but true, is the fact that the children of our nation are being filled with the garbage of Beverly Hills and Hollywood. How tragic it is that the average child in the USA "will have seen an average of eight thousand murders and one hundred thousand acts of violence," *before he finishes elementary school.* Let's take a look at just a couple examples of the repugnant "rubbish" Americans are feeding their souls within our present day:

❑ An episode of CBS's *Picket Fence, airing* just in time for Christmas, revolved around a crazed Christian gynecologist trying to bring about a type of virgin birth. He artificially inseminated a virgin with his own semen.

❑ A couple of episodes of Fox Network's *Martin* featured a pimp-turned-preacher, Leon Lonnie Love. But he still "behaves like a pimp." When asked by his date about the source of his money, he responded, "God does provide, God provides like a son of a [expletive deleted]."[251]

According to Greg Lewis in a very descriptive article entitled, "Telegarbage":

At the same time that TV emphasizes these [materialistic and glitzy] values, it ignores many values that the Bible teaches. On TV, there seems to be no such thing as sin. Almost the only people who believe in God are from another time in history – like the *Walton's* or the family in *Little House on the Prairie* [or more recently *Christy*]. It's as if God and His guidelines didn't even exist today.[252]

So much more could be said, but you get the point!

About half the children in our nation will spend at least part of their childhood in a single parent home, and the number is rising daily. As one author put it, "[I] magine a world where most children have several "moms" and "dads," perhaps six or eight "grand parents," and dozens of half-siblings. Little boys and girls will be shuffled to and fro in an ever-changing pattern of living arrangements. It doesn't take a child psychologist to realize that this type of environment will be, and already is, devastating to children."[253]

Over 600,000 teenage girls get pregnant each year, more than nine out of 10 of these are unmarried. Half of these terminate the pregnancy with an abortion.[254] Eighty-two percent of teens have had sexual relations by the age of 19. Seventy-five percent of all teens say that there is no such thing as absolute moral truth.[255] Forty percent of thirteen to seventeen year olds have watched a pornographic movie.[256] Thirty-five percent of fifteen-year-old boys and 27 percent of fifteen-year-old girls have had sex (an increase of 19 percent since 1982).[257]

Even more disturbing is the fact that among sexually active teenage girls, 60 percent have had multiple partners.[258] Twenty percent of teenagers will have had sex with at least four partners before they graduate.[259]

As one has noted, "A nation without morality cannot have morale." Could this be the reason that we have recently been informed that 75 percent of our young men are unwilling to go to war for our country? For the past forty years, we have been sowing. It is time to reap the harvest. Much like Rome of old, we have "ceased to be good" and the inevitable result is we "must cease to be great."

- CHAPTER 8 -

AMERICAN HOLOCAUST

*"For thou hast possessed my reins: thou hast covered me in my
mother's womb. I will praise thee; for I am fearfully and
wonderfully made: marvelous are thy works; and that my soul
knoweth right well. My substance was not hid from thee, when I
was made in secret, and curiously wrought in the lowest parts
of the earth."*

- Psalms 139:13-15

A bortion. No other word is as likely to divide friend and family members. There are few, if any, political issues more controversial than abortion. "Nonetheless, with the possible exception of Red China, the U.S. has the most liberal abortion laws in the world."[260] As many have noted, abortion is the number one moral issue of our day.

Nearly thirty years ago, our Supreme Court overturned all state laws (a violation of our Constitution) that protected children in the womb and legalized the "murder" of American children. Concerning abortion and the constitution, Robert Bork writes:

> I objected to Roe v. Wade ... because the decision was a radical deformation of the Constitution. The Constitution has nothing to say about abortion, leaving it, like most subjects, to the judgment and moral sense of the American people and their elected officials.[261]

Thus, a liberal ruling by the highest court in our nation made **murder** a "Constitutional right." As one author so aptly noted:

> According to the book of Judges, unrestrained homosexual perversion led to a civil war between the tribe of Benjamin and the rest of Israel. This civil war was actually fought over gay rights and altogether cost the lives of more than sixty-five thousand Benjaminites and Israelites (Judges 19 & 20).
>
> However in America, it hasn't been the unrestrained homosexual perversion but unrestrained heterosexual perversion, which has caused a civil war- a civil war against our unborn citizens by abortion! Whereas the civil war in Israel was fought over gay rights, the civil war in America is being fought over mother's rights.
>
> Furthermore, the death toll during Israel's gay rights civil war pales in comparison to the estimated thirty-eight million potential citizens who have died in the mother's rights civil war by abortion in America.[262]

Pro-Abortion or more appropriately, **"pro-death"** advocates promote a woman's right to choose. This group insists upon the right to an abortion on demand. They insist that a woman has the right to an abortion in the event of pregnancy as a result of rape and incest. Unfortunately, the child has no say in the matter!

But it doesn't stop there – they also believe that the woman has the right to abort the child who may be born with a deformity. Moreover, they also claim that a woman has the right to "kill" her child if the pregnancy is an inconvenience. It is a fact that "abortions in the United States for rape, incest, to protect the life of the mother, or to void a defective fetus comprise of less than **five percent** of all abortions."[263]

Nearly thirty percent of all American pregnancies are ended by abortions. Over 1.5 million children are slaughtered every year in the United States of America, and over 1.4 million of them are murdered for the sake of "convenience." Our country has lost more lives at the hands of the murderous physicians than by the weapons of military enemies. According to *Life Messengers*: "Total military losses of the United States in World War II were less than one-half million dead. But today over one million babies (actually 1.5 million) are murdered by abortion every year."[264]

Because so many American children are being "terminated" prematurely each year, the value of God-given life has been cheapened. Men have placed themselves in the place of God, deciding who has "quality of life" and the right to live. As one author so aptly put it, "Abortion, infanticide, and euthanasia are but dominoes in a line; abortion has fallen, infanticide is tottering, and euthanasia may soon follow."[265] The evidence is out. Since the 1973 Supreme Court decision allowing abortion on demand, respect for human life has diminished as Ronald Reagan and other warned it would.

Our nation has been "butchering" unborn children over the last three decades, thus becoming a cruel and uncivilized nation that has turned its back upon God and His Word. According to *World* magazine, January 16, 1999:

> Over the last several decades American doctors (in the name of "freedom of choice") have "dismembered or chemically burned" thirty-eight (the number is over 40 million now) million unborn babies to death.[266]

This number far exceeds the number of Russians killed by Stalin, Jews killed by Hitler, Cambodians killed by Pol Pot, or the number of Americans that have died in our many wars and conflicts over the past two hundred years. In other words, over the last several decades our physicians, who have taken an oath to help not hurt humanity, have systematically butchered nearly forty million children, a figure that "is so huge that it approximates the **combined** populations of twenty-four states. In fact, the number of babies aborted in the United States exceeds the entire population of Canada (population 27,296,859 – according to the 1991 Canadian census, p. 114)."[267]

As Americans, we have been astonished, appalled and we have agonized over the tragedy on September 11, 2001. And so we should. Nevertheless, it would take over twelve thousand September 11 tragedies to come up with a body count of forty million children. As John Warwick Montgomery pointed out: "If God did not tolerate the Nazi extermination of six million Jews, what makes us think that He will continue to ignore our mounting toll of infanticides?"[268]

ABORTION AND THE CHURCH

As author Dr. Phil Stringer declares, "Abortion cannot be reconciled with Christianity." He continues by saying, "The most serious advocates of abortion recognize that they are campaigning against basic Christian teaching."[269] Malcolm Potts wrote in a 1970 issue of *California Medicine Magazine*:

It will become necessary and acceptable to place relative rather than absolute values on such things as human lives ...This is quite distinctly at variance with the Judeo-Christian ethic and carries serious philosophical, social, economic, and political implications for Western society and perhaps for world society.

The process of eroding the old ethic and substituting the new has already begun. It may be seen clearly in the changing attitudes toward human abortion. In defiance of the long held Western ethic of intrinsic and equal values of every human life, regardless of its stage, condition, or status, abortion is becoming accepted by

146

society as moral, right and even necessary. It is worth noting that *this shift in public attitude has affected the churches, the laws, and the public policy rather than the reverse.*[270]

In other words the pro-death crowd has been more influential than the church, the Congress and our communities in general. Not to mention, the impact abortions have upon the church and our country more specifically. The supposed "Right to Choose" has diminished not only the "Right to Life," but also human life in general. United States Senator, Jesse Helms, wrote in his book, *When Free Men Shall Stand*:

> In the meantime, we must not lose sight of the anomaly, the odd spectacle that now exists in our country – where there is strong agitation to make tough laws protecting the wolves and where it is already a federal offense to destroy an eagle's egg and where all protection has been forfeited on unborn life.[271]

I believe we would all agree with the words of author Austin Sorenson who wrote in his book *Is America Committing Suicide?*, "What happened to our sense of values? Has human life become so cheap? How inconsistent we are! Isn't it strange? With a genuine concern over child abuse, America is moving rapidly to curb the discipline of children. Spankings will probably be illegal. Yet it is legal to kill unborn infants. 'Consistency, thou art a jewel!'"[272]

Our nation has acted barbaric and paganistic since *Roe v. Wade* in 1973 by butchering the helpless unborn citizens of America. Someone has said that abortion is "the number one moral issue of our day."[273] Former U.S. Surgeon General, Dr. C. Everett Koop made this observation, "... in a sinful world, liberty leads to license. If the law does not protect the life of an unborn baby, where will this lead? It will lead to infanticide and euthanasia among other things."[274] Of course, now with partial-birth abortion "infanticide" has arrived.

147

Another author once wrote, "To further New Age globalism, the Judeo-Christian ethic with its celebration of life must be effectively undermined. No doubt *Roe v. Wade* has dramatically altered the moral fabric of American society, and that of the world at large. This comes at a price."[275] She continues by saying:

> Whenever, contrary to the plan of God, human life is perceived as expendable, the enemy is released to carry out his counterfeit plan which circumvents the "abundant life" Jesus promised.[276]

During the Clinton administration, Alan Keyes, former ambassador to the U.N. Economic and Social Council, wrote in his book *Our Character, Our Nation*: "I wonder if Mrs. Clinton understands, for instance, the intimate connection between violence on the streets and violence against the unborn in the womb?"[277] Keyes also made an indicting statement about the Clinton administration when he said:

> ... Judging by the Clinton administration's policies on abortion and sex education, I doubt it. President Clinton is pro-choice. He supports a position that encourages young women to believe it's better to take a human life than to take personal responsibility for the consequences of their actions. Ultimately, the pro-choice position rests on the notion that there is no law respecting life that is higher than personal convenience and gratification.[278]

Keyes correctly perceives that the abortion "position is related to the 'safe-sex' condom distribution approach to sex education. This approach assumes that there are certain animal passions that people, and especially young people, simply can't control."[279] He continues by saying, "They're all going to do it, so we just have to get them to do it safely. Forget the fact that the 'safe sex, safer sex' slogan is a dangerous myth (Russian roulette is arguably safer than suicide, but do we distribute pamphlets recommending it to people suffering depression?).

Forget the notion that human beings have a rational will strong enough to control our animal desires."[280]

Concerning the travesty and tragedy of abortion, Jack Kemp once said:

> Every single year, there is a tragic silence of a million newborn cries that will never be developed; Potential we will never see; Books never authored; Inventions never made ... the right to life is a gift from God, not a gift of the state.[281]

Professor L.R. Agnew of the UCLA School of Medicine relates the story of when he posed this question to his students:

> Here is the family history. The father has syphilis. The mother has tuberculosis. They have already had four children. The first one is blind, the second one died. The third child is deaf. The fourth also has tuberculosis.
>
> The mother is pregnant with her fifth child. The parents are willing to have an abortion if you decide they should. What do you think? Most of the students decided on abortion.
>
> "Congratulations! You have just murdered Beethoven."[282]

The sobering truth is "30 percent of all babies conceived in this country are killed before they see the light of day." It is reported that in certain cities in America there are "more abortions than live births ... At this rate, we will soon have to apologize to Adolph Hitler"[283]

As with just about everything else, following the money trail will help us to see the "importance" of abortion to business. News commentator, Tom Anderson wrote:

> Murdering babies is now big business. In effect, the mushrooming of abortion clinics' advertisement might read like this: "Have your baby murdered while you wait!" "Kill now, pay later." ... "Ask about our special lay-away plan."[284]

149

MYTHS THAT MURDER

Dr. Phil Stringer has written an excellent book called *The Transformation: America's Journey Toward Darkness*; in this book he lists various myths concerning abortion. Myth number 4, as found in his book, is that **THE VAST MAJORITY OF AMERICANS SUPPORT ABORTION.** As Dr. Stringer points out, "If you ask Americans if they approve of abortion as a method of birth control, a clear majority say no. If you ask Americans if they think abortions should be taxpayer-funded, an overwhelming majority is clearly opposed."[285] Dr. Stringer correctly perceives and continues by saying:

> The issue of public support ... is a false one. If a majority of people supported slavery, would that make it right? If a majority wanted to practice genocide against the Jews, would that make it right?

> Our founders wanted some clear laws that would protect minorities from the whims of the majority. They clearly determined that protecting the "right to life" was one of the unalterable purposes of government. The right to life is not based upon a majority decision; it is a God-given right.[286]

Another myth Dr. Stringer brings out in his book is the myth that **WOMEN HAVE A CONSTITUTIONAL RIGHT TO ABORTION.** Cited in his book are the following words from a discussion of the *Human Life Amendment*, which the *Religious Coalition for Abortion Rights* ran an ad for. The ad stated:

> Right now the United States Senate is holding hearings on a Constitutional Amendment to outlaw abortion. This effort, backed by a handful of Senators, seriously threatens the religious freedom of every American. If they succeed, you will be forced to accept, as law, one narrow religious and moral belief–even if it is not your own, your church's, or your synagogue's.

150

We believe abortion is an individual decision and, therefore, your God-given right. While we support a woman's choice to become a mother, we also support her choice not to. But most importantly, we feel no religious group has the right to use the power of politics to impose their beliefs on you.

Yet this is precisely what the Constitutional Amendment would do. By outlawing abortion, it will rob you of the right to make your most personal decisions according to your own conscience. By your support of the Religious Coalition for Abortion Rights, we can work together to stop this small group from forcing you to practice what they preach.[287]

JUDGMENT IS COMING

In spite of the fact that our nation has turned its back on defending the "rights" and protecting the life of the child in the womb, each child killed is special to God. The Psalmist made this clear when he said, *"Lo, children are an heritage of the Lord: and the fruit of the womb is his reward"* (Psalms 127:3). God blesses us with children, but we "literally throw His children, by the millions, in the garbage."[288] The Scriptures are clear that God's judgment is upon the nation that sheds the blood of its innocent children.

Ezekiel 36:16-18, "Moreover the word of the LORD came unto me, saying, Son of man, when the house of Israel dwelt in their own land, they defiled it by their own way and by their doings: their way was before me as the uncleanness of a removed woman. Wherefore I poured my fury upon them for the blood that they had shed upon the land, and for their idols wherewith they had polluted it ..."

Proverbs 6:16-18, "These six things doth the LORD hate: yea, seven are an abomination unto him: A proud look, a lying tongue, and hands that shed innocent blood, An heart that deviseth wicked imaginations, feet that be swift in running to mischief ..."

151

As Abel's blood cried out to God (Genesis 4:10), so the blood of forty million butchered children cry out to God. As one author declared, "The voice of their shed blood must be a deafening roar to God. Their voices cry out for justice."[289]

As we learn in the Old Testament, the shedding of innocent blood and flagrant immorality brought the wrath of a Holy God down upon the Amorites. These same sins can be found in America today. For over 400 years, God tried to stop the Amorites from sacrificing their children, but eventually only His judgment would bring an end to their wicked ways. The Amorites were an extremely violent people and God would use violence to end their violence. The principle of "sowing and reaping" is inevitable. If judgment hasn't already come, it must be right around the corner.

> *Galatians 6:7-8,* "*Be not deceived; God is not mocked: for whatsoever a man soweth, that shall he also reap. For he that soweth to his flesh shall of the flesh reap corruption; but he that soweth to the Spirit shall of the Spirit reap life everlasting.*"

The Scriptures also record for us the history of ancient Israel. They too ignored God's commands about the shedding of innocent blood like the Amorites. God sent prophet after prophet for hundreds of years in an attempt to bring Israel back to their "spiritual senses" and to stop them from shedding innocent blood, but Israel's heart became harder and harder against the will and Word of God. Notice this indictment found in the May 1980 *Moody Monthly* in an editorial entitled, "What Ever Happened to the Evangelical?"

> Could it be that ours is a generation more wicked than any other that has lived upon the earth? By comparison, the Crusaders, Inquisitors, even the Nazis, were minor leaguers. They destroyed children and adults committed to an ideology. We destroy the unborn ... The United States Supreme Court has given women the

right to abortion on demand, making the casual destruction of the unborn the law of the land.[290]

This was written over twenty years ago, and folks, we are far more vile and wicked than they were in 1980. God's Word makes it clear that an unborn child is a human being and that the blood of the slain innocent cries out for justice. Listen to the words of R.F.D. Gardner:

> The Old Testament reminds us that God is the giver of life, the One by whose power fetal development occurs, and to whom every living soul belongs. This being so, life is not to be taken on one's own initiative, not even for the most inescapable of obligations, the blood feud. Man is not to cause the death of the innocent and guiltless, for the blood of the innocent cries to God from the ground."[291]

The church of Jesus Christ has always (until recently) believed that abortion was murder because, "from conception the seed is a child."

> *Isaiah 44:24, "Thus saith the Lord, thy Redeemer, and He that formed thee from the womb, I am the Lord that maketh all things...."*

> *Jeremiah 1:4-5, "Then the word of the LORD came unto me, saying, Before I formed thee in the belly I knew thee; and before thou camest forth out of the womb I sanctified thee, and I ordained thee a prophet unto the nations."*

Early church father Tertullian wrote: "For us, murder is once-for-all forbidden; so even the child in the womb, while yet the mother's blood is being drawn on to form the human being, it is not lawful for us to destroy. To forbid birth is only quick murder. It makes no difference whether one takes away the life once born or destroys it as it comes to birth. He is a man, who is to be a man; the fruit is always present in the seed."[292]

The wholesale butchering of our young has resulted in producing a "reprobate" spirit in our nation and has, no doubt, forced God to withdraw His hand of blessing from America. As one author has noted, "You cannot give consent to abortion and still be moved by glory of American freedom." Why? Because our freedom was based upon the truth that all men are created equal ... with certain unalienable rights; that among these are *life*, liberty, and the pursuit of happiness.

Because we have denied these rights to over forty million children, "the basic meaning of our nation becomes tasteless, barren, and defunct," writes, Dr. R. L. Hymers, Jr. Hymers continues with the following:

> The hearts of our people died with those children, under the abortionist's knife. They may have continued living physically, but they committed spiritual suicide by condoning this Holocaust. They live on like zombies – shuffling across the land of the living dead.[293]

The clouds of judgment hang over this country as we turn our heads to the abomination known as abortion. It is time that the church of Jesus Christ rise up and shine the light of God's Word upon this abominable act being committed – nearly 5,000 each day. Our pulpits can no longer be silent concerning the "butchering" of the unborn children. Someone has been quoted as saying:

> Once the United States was known as the world's chief advocate of dignity, the sanctity, and the inherent rights of each human life. Once we were the world's leading defender of every human being's right to life, liberty, and the pursuit of happiness. We are losing ground in all three of those inherent rights, but in none so much as in the defense of the right of human beings to live.[294]

In the words of one author, "America is acting like a pagan nation. God has judged America for killing unborn babies." The murder of unborn infants, writes Sorenson, "may be the 'last straw' with our Maker. As some have pointed out, such action may be the turning point of our history – it could be the point of 'no return.'"[295]

"Whoever wishes to ruin a nation has only to get the vice of sodomy introduced. For it is extremely difficult to excavate it, where it has once taken root and once it has footing in any country, however powerful and flourishing we may venture as politicians to predict that the foundation of its future decline is laid, and that after some hundred years it will no longer be the same powerful country it is at present."

-SIR JOHN DAVID MCCALISS

- CHAPTER 9 -

HOMOSEXUALITY IN AMERICA

An Abomination or An Alternative Lifestyle?

"Thou shalt not lie with mankind, as with womankind: it is abomination. Neither shalt thou lie with any beast to defile thyself therewith: neither shall any woman stand before a beast to lie down thereto: it is confusion. Defile not ye yourselves in any of these things: for in all these the nations are defiled which I cast out before you: And the land is defiled: therefore I do visit the iniquity thereof upon it, and the land itself vomiteth out her inhabitants."

- Leviticus 18:22-30

One of the great abominations of our day is the open acceptance and tolerance of homosexuality. Just a few weeks ago, here in my hometown of Long Beach, California, well over 100,000 gays, lesbians and gay/lesbian sympathizers showed up for the annual gay and lesbian parade.

The foundation of our nation is being destroyed and the biblical pattern of the family has come under a barrage of attacks from many different and destructive ideologies. There is none more godless than the homosexual agenda that is permeating and polluting our nation – right before our eyes! In the Christian biblical value system – homosexuality is a sin. The supposed "gay" lifestyle is not simply an alternative lifestyle, but rather an abominable lifestyle, which God abhors.

157

As a matter of fact, it is the only sin mentioned in the Scriptures that makes the land itself vomit.

> *1 Corinthians 6:9-11, Know ye not that the unrighteous shall not inherit the kingdom of God? Be not deceived: neither fornicators, nor idolaters, nor adulterers, nor effeminate, nor abusers of themselves with mankind, nor thieves, nor covetous, nor drunkards, nor revilers, nor extortioners, shall inherit the kingdom of God. And such were some of you: but ye are washed, but ye are sanctified, but ye are justified in the name of the Lord Jesus, and by the Spirit of our God.*

Homosexuality is almost as old as mankind. Of course, the first mention of it in recorded history concerns Lot and the well-known cities of Sodom and Gomorrah, well over 4,000 years ago. Certainly there have been homosexuals in our nation from its very conception, but the militant and open flaunting of this perversion is a relatively recent development. Nowhere has the sixties generation's bequeathing of sexual license been more evident than in the gay rights movement.

BLASPHEMOUS MYTHS

As author Dr. Phil Stringer points out in his book *The Transformation: America's Journey Towards Darkness*, there are some basic myths concerning homosexuality that have permeated our society and polluted our mindset concerning the topic. Adolph Hitler once said, "If you repeat a lie long enough and loud enough people will believe it."

We will consider only two, the two that have really taken hold in the average American mindset today. The most common myth in regards to homosexuality is *HOMOSEXUALITY IS GENETIC*. Homosexuals are working tirelessly "at spreading this myth," writes Dr. Stringer. But study after study and the Holy Scriptures all confirm the falsehood of this myth. In the words of Dr. Charles Wahl, "The vast preponderance of evidence clearly indicates that homosexuality *is a learned disorder* and is not genetically inherited."[296] Dr. Stringer reminds us:

> Homosexual activists are fond of quoting a few "scientific studies" conducted by homosexual activists, which are said to indicate the possibility of genetic factors relating to homosexuality. Despite the fact that these studies were conducted by activists without academic qualifications, without normal guidelines and control groups, and without observation or verification of results, activists are quick to accept them and promote their purported results. The news media and some politicians are also quick to accept these studies and quote them as if they are proven scientific facts. The truth is, these studies are based more upon wishful thinking than any scientific results.[297]

A great majority of Americans today do not believe that gays can control their homosexual desires because they were born homosexual. This mistaken philosophy makes God out to be a liar. The Scriptures are clear that God will never allow us to be tempted to sin above our ability to endure. It is written:

> *1 Corinthians 10:13b, "... God is faithful, who will not suffer you to be tempted above that which ye are able; but will with the temptation also make a way of escape, that ye may be able to bear it.*

Another myth being pushed on our society is that *10 PERCENT OF THE AMERICAN PEOPLE ARE HOMOSEXUAL*. It is upon this myth that much of the homosexual agenda is being promoted in the nation's government-run public school system. This myth is based upon Kinsey's 1948 book *Sexual Behavior in the American Male*. In this book which, along with his other works, literally transformed our culture into a sinful and sex-crazed society, Kinsey claimed that 4 percent of the male population is homosexual and that an additional six percent may, at one time or another, experiment with homosexuality.

Dr. Judith Reisman in her book *Kinsey: Crimes & Consequences* informs us, not only of Kinsey's corrupt lifestyle, but also of his faulty research that led to his supposed 10 percent theory. It's a lie and much of America has fallen for it, hook line and sinker. The fact is, depending on which studies you want to take as "gospel," no more than 1 to 3 percent of America's population are homosexual.

Despite the fact that the latest studies and statistics reject Kinsey's earlier inaccurate estimates that claimed 10 percent of the population is homosexual, the propaganda war fought by the perverted gay and lesbian lobbyists has been enduring and effective.

Nevertheless, it wouldn't matter if 90 percent of Americans were homosexual, that isn't the issue. The issue, of course, is what does God say! As author David James King, M.D. stated:

> In other words, no one is genetically programmed at birth ... to commit homosexual sins. Therefore, the gay male is not born to be a homosexual, any more than the heterosexual male is born to be an adulterer or a rapist, or the poor man is born a rapist. So in God's mind, the homosexual should always be held responsible ... for the sins of homosexuality.[298]

DESENSITIZATION OF AMERICA

The homosexuals are using every means possible to desensitize the American people concerning homosexuality. Listen to this quote from an article published in a 1987 Guide magazine entitled *The Overhauling of Straight America*:

> The first order of business is desensitization of the American public concerning gays and gay rights. To desensitize the public is to help it view homosexuality with indifference instead of with keen emotion.

In just over a decade, the gay movement has achieved this goal. Alan Keyes, former ambassador to the U.N. understood the predicament clearly when he wrote: "Homosexuals today are not just insisting that other people leave them alone. They are insisting that others respect them." He continues, "Yet as many Christians read the Bible, the biblical God declares unequivocally, 'Thou shalt not lie with mankind as with womankind: It is an abomination.' According to their religion, homosexuality cannot be respected; it must be condemned. People who practice homosexuality reject the Bible command that condemns it."

As Keyes notes, the government has "no right to tell Bible-believing Christians that they must violate their religious conscience by respecting what the Bible condemns, or allowing their children to be educated in doctrines that contradict their biblical beliefs. If we use state power to enforce the view that homosexuality cannot be condemned, or public money to finance educational programs aimed at encouraging respect for homosexuality, we will be doing just that."[299]

THE MEDIA'S GAY AGENDA

"In other words, it's beginning to look like all these new gay characters suddenly springing up on the airwaves aren't entirely accidental. It's beginning to look like TV has an agenda. A gay agenda!"[300]

More than anywhere else, the assault of homosexual propaganda is found in the entertainment industry and the education systems of our nation. Of course, the reasoning behind this is to influence those who are most impressionable – the youth of our nation.

Ellen (degenerate) DeGeneres rocked the nation by coming out of the closet. "Ellen was the show that first kicked open the door for gay TV."[301] Today, gay characters are so common on television, so unexotic, that their sexual orientation has become all but invisible to most viewers. It is, in a sense, the ultimate sign of *acceptance* and *tolerance*. "Here's how far we've come in the last five years," says *Will & Grace's* co-creator David Kohan, "The question networks used to ask was whether their shows had too many gay plotlines in them. Today, they ask whether they have too many gay shows."[302]

According to *Entertainment* magazines special report "Gay Hollywood" *Normal, Ohio*, starred John Goodman as a gay father. Today, we have gay TV doctors (*Chicago Hope & ER*), gay police-precinct workers (*NYPD Blue*), gay killers (*HBO's Oz*), gay teens (*Dawson's Creek and Buffy the Vampire Slayer*), gay students (*Felicity*), gay political aides (*Spin City*), gay TV executives (*Showtime's Beggars and Choosers*), gay cartoon dogs (*South Park*), even gay game show winners (*Survivor*) and their partners (with *Who Wants to Be A Millionaire's* cameras zooming in on them as Regis Philbin greets them in the studio audience).

Will & Grace's other co-creator, Mark Mutchnick (who happens to be gay) declared that "Television is a pretty accurate reflection of society as a whole and stereotypes just don't work anymore. Forget offensive – they're just not believable. They don't ring true. Gay stereotypes on TV today would be like black stereotypes. Nobody would buy it. The world has changed."[303] No doubt about that – "The world has changed," *but we must not change with the world.*

Again according to *Entertainment* magazine's special report, "there's more happening here than TV casting a cathode-ray reflection of society. Attitudes about gays have shifted in the past five years ... and certainly not without TV's help. In fact, television today seems to be championing gay rights in much the same way it fostered civil rights in the 1960's and 1970's. During that tumultuous time TV was used to change America's hearts and minds about race..."[304] The report goes on to say, "In other words, it's beginning to look like all these new gay characters suddenly springing up on the airwaves aren't entirely accidental. It's beginning to look like TV has an agenda. *A gay agenda!*[305]

Kevin Williamson, creator of the teen drama *Dawson's Creek*, which became the first network TV series in history to show two teenage boys romantically kissing said, "I remember the first time I was exposed to gay people on TV. It was *Family...* It was big back then. Pretty amazing. We've come a long way since I was a kid."[306] The article continues by saying: *"While Hollywood has always been accepting of gay talent – at least behind the camera – it's never before been so enthusiastically embracing."*[307]

Brian Graden, the (gay) president of programming for MTV, a network that's long included gay themes in its mix said, "It's a generational thing." Each generation pushes things a little further. The kid's growing up now, they'll push things even more when they grow up."[308] The article goes on to admit, "TV is the idea medium for pushing things, even more so than feature films." They recognize the power of influence that a gay character has over a period of time. According to *Emmy* winner Holland:

> There's less risk on TV, so you have more freedom. A gay character in 22 hours [of a TV show] is not as important as a gay character in a two-hour movie. You aren't risking you're entire box office by having a gay character.[309]

According to Max Mutchnick there has been a "lack of outrage" over Will & Grace. He says, "The story behind the story is that there has been absolutely no controversy about our show. People seem to be responding to the characters, not their sexual orientations."[310]

Multitudes are watching these shows. According to *Entertainment*, "Even in summer reruns, *Will & Grace* – which *NBC* sometimes aired twice a week- regularly attracted 10 million viewers ... And there you have it- the real reason for the increasing number of gay shows on TV: They're starting to make money."[311] According to the article:

> After decades of being marginalized, demonized, or completely ignored, gays have finally found their way onto mainstream TV by becoming the most powerful of special interest groups: an audience demographic. Or at least a coveted part of the most coveted demographic, 18 to 49 year olds with lots of disposable income.[312]

As Bible believing Christians it is imperative that we **reject** the idea that one can be a "spirit-filled" and "spirit-controlled" Christian and a practicing homosexual. We must also **resist** the attempts that are being made in our nation to normalize or legalize homosexuality. In light of the growth of the gay and lesbian movement in the United States, it would be to our benefit to understand what God has to say about homosexuality. As Bible believing Christians we cannot or should not be deceived into accepting these godless myths that are being promoted on a daily basis in our nation.

When God created the world, He established fundamental distinctions between – *"male and female"* (Genesis 1:27). It was God's plan from the very beginning for sexual relations to be in the form of a man and woman relationship with the two becoming *"one flesh"* (Genesis 2:24). Genesis records the story of Adam and Eve, not Adam and Steve. Oh, I almost forgot – homosexuality is mentioned in Genesis, the seed book of the Bible. It's found in Genesis 19 – the story of Sodom and Gomorrah.

Because we have refused to "outlaw and punish sexual immorality," especially the sin of homosexuality, this godless abomination has moved "from the darkness into the light until aberration becomes acceptable and sodomy becomes the standard."[313] Homosexuals and their defenders, who argue that all human beings have the right to self-understanding and expression, reflect their determination to reject and replace God's way for their vile and wicked ways. God's Word is very clear concerning the act of homosexuality. We are warned that men are not to *"lie with mankind, as with womankind: it is an abomination"* (Leviticus 18:22).

God also says "If a man also lie with mankind, as he lieth with a woman, both of them have committed an abomination: they shall surely be put to death; their blood shall be upon them" (Leviticus 20:13). In Romans chapter one, inspired by God, Paul teaches us that God's wrath is revealed from heaven against those who participate in the ungodly sin of homosexuality. According the great apostle, homosexuality is the cultural culmination of defiant rebellion against a holy God. It is also symptomatic of a corrupt society that is under the judgment of God.

PROMISCUITY AND PERVERSENESS

No only is homosexuality a sin, but it is a deviant sickness. According to Romans chapter one, homosexuality is the result of being given over to a "reprobate" mind. Promiscuity among homosexuals "is unbelievable to those uninformed on the subject."[314] Read the statistics and judge for yourself. Dr. Monteith states:

> Studies show that male homosexuals average between 20 and 106 partners **every year**. The average homosexual has 300 to 500 partners in his lifetime. Thirty-seven percent engage in sadomasochism, at least 28 percent have engaged in sodomy with more than a thousand men. ... Compared to heterosexuals, male homosexuals are ... 5,000 times more likely to have contacted AIDS.[315]

Concerned Women for America's study *"The Homosexual Deception: Making Sin A Civil Right,"* has informed us that homosexual "AIDS victims in this study averaged more than 1,100 lifetime sexual partners. Some reported as many as 20,000."[316]

Even in Dr. Kinsey's 1948 report, which the gays quote as "holy writ," when it comes to the study's inaccurate number of 10 percent of the country being homosexual, the perverseness of the homosexual life-style is revealed. In perhaps the most thorough study of homosexual behavior ever undertaken, published by the Kinsey Institute in Bell and Weinberg's book, *Homosexuality, A study of Diversity Among Men and Women*, we learn that:

❑ 43 percent of white male homosexuals estimated that they had sex with 500 or more different partners. 75 percent had 100 or more. 28 percent reported more than 1000 partners.

❑ 79 percent said that more than half of their partners were strangers.

❑ 70 percent said more than half their sexual partners were men with whom they had sex only once.[317]

One author warns us, "Just as unrestrained heterosexual perversion increases the frequency of fornication, adultery, rape, and gang rape, so also unrestrained homosexual perversion increases the frequency of homosexuality, homosexual rape and homosexual gang rape."[318]

HOMOSEXUALITY AND THE CHILDREN

The gay movement "is forthright about seeking to legitimize child-adult homosexual sex."[319] In 1980 the largest Dutch gay organization "adopted the position that the liberation of pedophilia must be viewed as a gay issue... [and that] ages of consent should therefore be abolished ... by acknowledging the affinity between homosexuality and pedophilia," they have "made it easier for homosexual adults to become more sensitive to erotic desires of younger members of their sex, therefore broadening gay identity."[320]

One survey by two homosexual authors found that 73 percent of homosexuals had at some time had sex with boys 16-19 years old or younger.[321] In spite of the fact that study after study has yielded estimates of male homosexuality that range between 1 percent and 3 percent, yet they account for anywhere between 20 percent and 40 percent of all child molestations.[322] According to the reports the risk of "a homosexual molesting a child is 10 to 20 times greater than that of a heterosexual."[323]

In the U.S. and Canada, the *North American Man-Boy Love Association* march proudly in many gay pride parades with the stated goal of removing the barriers to man-boy sex.[324] According to J.C. Coleman, in Abnormal Psychology and Modern Life, "more than 50 percent of adult homosexuals had been seduced by older homosexuals before the age of 14."[325]

REDEFINING THE FAMILY

Alvin Toffler states that "a bewildering array of family forms: homosexual marriages, communes, groups of elderly people banding together to share expenses (and sometimes sex), tribal grouping among certain ethnic minorities, and many other forms coexist as never before."[326]

The following from a *CFV Report*, Colorado for Family Values, January 1995, gives us a glimpse of some true homosexual thinking. "A middle ground might be to fight for same-sex marriage and its benefits and then, once granted, **redefine the institution of marriage completely** ... to debunk a myth and radically altar an archaic institution that as it now stands keeps us down. The most subversive action lesbian and gay men can undertake ... is to transform the notion of the family entirely."[327]

Now we have the abhorrent Rosie O'Donnell taking up the "standard" for homosexual adoptions. According to the *Washington Times*, "No one knows how many children have been adopted by homosexual parents. Estimates run from 1 million to 14 million."[328] **"Repulsive Rosie"** is becoming a heroine to many of the children in America; she was recently on **NICKELODEON** pushing her wicked wares. What will be the next step in this godless movement's agenda?

In the May 2000 issue of "Demography," published by the Population Association of America, researcher Dan Black estimated that 3.9 percent of the population is homosexual, and that 21.7 percent of lesbian couples and 5.2 percent of homosexual male couples have children in the home.[329] According to Dr. Paul Cameron's *Family Research Report* "children are increasingly being given to homosexuals and lesbians when their custody is being disputed by a heterosexual parent."[330] This should be frightening, states one author, "when surveys of homosexuals show that nearly 25 percent of them say they enjoy sex with children."[331]

According to Laura McAlpine, executive director of the Women's Health Center in Chicago, "70 percent of the women applying for artificial insemination are lesbians." The first seminar on lesbian parenting held in Chicago in 1992 was filled to capacity, according to an article in Concerned Women for America's *Issues at a Glance*.[332]

Acts of public sodomy, once a crime meriting capital punishment in America, are becoming prevalent, particularly during the "gay pride" marches in the larger cities. "The North American Man-Boy Love Association now marches proudly in gay parades, meets in public buildings, and publishes reports on how to coerce young children into sexual acts," writes Kevin Swanson.[333]

In the early 1990's Dr. Edward Brongersma, wrote: "In a recently published French study, 129 men (average age 34 years old) said they had had sex with a total of 11,007 boys (an average of 85 boys per man).[334] "... At the University of California, 30 percent of the male and 35 percent of the female students reported having had at least one sexual contact with an adult."[335]

THE PUBLIC SCHOOL SYSTEM'S GAY AGENDA

One of the key battlegrounds for the homosexuals is found on the public school campus. In an effort to help "sexually diverse" students cope, homosexual speakers are explicitly recruiting students in the classroom, informing the students that

10 percent of them are gay and must learn to acknowledge that they cannot change this "fact" of nature.

As we mentioned earlier, the fact of the matter concerning the "10 percent" theory that originated with Kinsey's studies is that it has been thoroughly rejected since it was made widely known that his studies were not conducted on a scientific, random population. In fact, his findings were based on a study of convicts (many of them pedophiles and rapists).[336] As one author has stated, "The NEA has a captive audience of children and it's planning to use that power to force-feed those children the homosexual agenda."

Children and teens are not only being provided with "hot line" phone numbers that will offer homosexual sensitive counseling, but also "sensitivity" counseling on many government-run school campuses. All students are pressured to accept homosexuality as a natural alternative life-style, even if it violates the rights and religious beliefs or moral values, and homosexual students are being given special treatment. Some of the curriculum "urges educators to teach that homosexuality and lesbianism are acceptable life-styles (like being left-handed) ..."[337] Sadly, the message infiltrating our schools about homosexuality is far from balanced and factual ... It is biased and pushes an agenda seeking to reshape our children's values.

Virginia Uribe, founder of *Project 10*, a homosexual recruitment program that had its roots in Los Angeles and has now been adopted by the NEA nationally says, "you can't allow public opinion to dictate what you do—instead you must mold public opinion."[338] Schools are being flooded with literature, videos, and testimonials advocating the pro-gay perspective in public education ... the one-sided message that students should explore and embrace their homosexual desires. Gay activists may claim that it is absurd to suspect there is any scheme to promote homosexuality, but the fact remains, they are working diligently to win "converts" to their perverted life-style.

Recognizing that parents would not stand for a direct push for acceptance of homosexuality, one gay former teacher explained, "We immediately seized upon the opponent's (parent's) calling card – safety." Safety is the Trojan horse for the acceptance of homosexuality. Rather than meaning protecting others and their views, they took the term and subtly changed its definition to embracing. As the pro-gay agenda is furthered upon the unsubstantiated grounds that homophobia is being eradicated, the acceptance of the normality of homosexuality becomes more prominent than ever.

According to the *Citizen* magazine, "In conjunction with the new laws, California's liberal Superintendent of Public Instruction Delaine Easton formed a 36-member advisory task force to translate them into state Education Codes. The task force, though billing itself as a champion of diversity – showed little diversity in its makeup. It was stacked with gay activists and sympathizers affiliated with such esoteric groups as *Older Asian Sisters in Solidarity* (OASIS) and *Lavender Youth Recreation and Information Center* (LYRIC) as well as more "mainstream" outfits like GLSEN and the *National Education Association Gay and Lesbian Caucus*." The article goes on to say, "On April 11, 2001, following months of closed-door meetings, the task force presented its recommendations in a 21-page report. They included:

❏ Surveying children to probe their attitudes about homosexuality.

❑ Integrating pro-homosexual and pro-transgender (yes, transgender) messages into "all" curricula, including science, history, language arts, and even math.

❑ Creating new policies "to reduce [the] adverse impact of gender segregation ... related to locker room facilities, restrooms and dress."

❑ Posting "positive grade level appropriate visual images" that include "all sexual orientations and gender identities" throughout the school.

❑ Using taxpayer dollars to establish Gay-Straight Alliances on campuses, put all school personnel through extensive and "ongoing" sensitivity training, pay for a media blitz, "provide rehabilitation to perpetrators" of discrimination and appoint a person in each school to monitor implementation of the new programs.

Karen Holgate, director of policy for the pro-family *Capitol Resource Institute*, says it adds up to "large-scale indoctrination." She adds:

> They clearly want all of our children to accept homosexuality as a positive, normal, healthy lifestyle, regardless of what their parents or the Bible or their churches might say. ... They're pitting the school and the state against the values and beliefs of parents.

This tolerance, of course, has touched every aspect of our society, including our school systems. Various programs that the NEA have already instituted and are working on instituting would occur without the consent of parents and takes the power from the parents to dictate what their children learn and when they learn it. Schools, not parents, would decide when and what the children learn about homosexuality. For more on the Gay Agenda in public education see our book *Temples of Darkness*.

A WORD FROM OUR HOMOSEXUAL FRIENDS:

This garbage was lifted from a Gay and Lesbian magazine. Let's wake up; they are out to capture the hearts and minds of our children and conquer the soul of our nation.

We shall sodomize your sons, emblems of your feeble masculinity, of your shallow dreams and vulgar lies. We will seduce them in your schools, in your dormitories, in your gymnasiums, in your locker rooms, in your sports arenas, in your seminaries, in your youth groups, in your movie theatre bathrooms, in your army bunkhouses, in your truck stops, in your all male clubs, in your houses of Congress, wherever men are with men together. Your sons will become our minions and do our bidding. They will be recast in our image. They will come to crave and adore us. ... All laws banning homosexual activity will be revoked. Instead legislation shall be passed which engenders love between men.

All homosexuals must stand together as brothers; we must be united artistically, philosophically, socially, politically and financially. We will triumph only when we present a common face to the vicious *heterosexual enemy*. If you dare cry faggot, fairy, queer, at us, we will stab you in your cowardly hearts and defile your dead puny bodies.

Our writers will make love between men fashionable and de rigueur, and we will succeed because we are adept at setting styles. We will eliminate heterosexual liaisons ... we will unmask the powerful homosexuals who masquerade as heterosexual. You will be shocked and frightened when you learn that your presidents and their sons, your industrialists, your senators, your mayors, your generals, your athletes, your film stars, your TV personalities, your civic leaders, your priests are not the safe, familiar bourgeois, heterosexual figures you assumed them to be. We are everywhere; we have infiltrated your ranks. Be careful when you speak of homosexuals because we are always among you ...

173

There will be no compromises. We are not middle class weaklings. Highly intelligent, we are the natural aristocrats of the human race, and steely-minded aristocrats never settle for less. Those who oppose us will be exiled. We shall raise vast, private armies, as Mishma did, to defeat you. We will conquer the world because warriors inspired by and banded together by homosexual love and honor are invincible as were the ancient Greek soldiers. The family unit – spawning ground of lies, betrayals, mediocrity, hypocrisy, and violence – will be abolished. The family unit, which only dampens imagination and curbs free will, must be eliminated. Perfect boys will be conceived and grown in the laboratory. They will be bonded together in communal setting, under the control and instruction of homosexual savants.

All churches [that] condemn us will be closed. Our only gods are handsome young men. ... Any man contaminated with heterosexual lust will be automatically barred from a position of influence. All males who insist on remaining stupidly heterosexual will be tried in homosexual courts of justice and will become invisible men.

We shall rewrite history, history filled and debased with your heterosexual lies and distortions. We shall portray the homosexuality of great leaders and thinkers who have shaped the world. We will demonstrate that homosexuality and intelligence and imagination are inextricably linked, and that homosexuality is a requirement for true nobility, true beauty in man. *We will be victorious* because we are filled with the ferocious bitterness of the oppressed ... We too are capable of firing guns and manning the barricades of the ultimate revolution.[339]

Folks, the radical homosexual recognizes that there is a battle for the soul of our nation and is willing to pay the price to be victorious. How about the church of Jesus Christ? Are we willing to pay the price for a victory?

Of course, the above individual is one "sick puppy." But don't think for a moment that he's alone in his perverted philosophical reasoning. A recent homosexual publication

174

blasphemed Christ, which is not uncommon. Robert Knight wrote the following in *The Kansas Christian*:

> The *Advocate* (gay magazine) front cover of December 13, 1994, asks, "Is God Gay?" and depicts Jesus Christ in garish colors as a homosexual, complete with sexual devices around his neck and obscene body-part imagery around and on Him,
>
> Inside the magazine is an even more obscene portrayal: a full color, full-page picture that includes realistic renderings of male and female genitalia. It accompanies a disingenuous article about the merits of the homosexual-oriented Metropolitan Community Church.[340]

THE DESTRUCTION OF OUR NATION

There are many educators, politicians and leaders in the gay movement who seek to advance the homosexual agenda in public schools and the public square, and in this they have been extremely successful. One of the surest ways for a nation to self-destruct is to allow homosexuality to gain acceptance. In 1814, Sir John David McCaliss did a comprehensive study on homosexuality in which he stated:

> Whoever wishes to ruin a nation has only to get the vice of sodomy introduced. For it is extremely difficult to excavate it, where it has once taken root and once it has footing in any country, however powerful and flourishing we may venture as politicians to predict that the foundation of its future decline is laid, and that after some hundred years it will no longer be the same powerful country it is at present.[341]

Dr. David James King said it well when he stated, "God's laws against homosexuality were designed to help not hurt us. They were designed to create wholesome, God-fearing, two-parent families (made up of one husband and one wife) that would fill the world with a godly seed." He continues with this warning:

> Christian society will inevitably lose the battle over "gay rights" because the moment we impertinently decided that God's laws were wrong and that these sins against God should no longer be punishable crimes, we lost the entire war. All that remains is when and how we will ultimately surrender.[342]

CRIMINALIZING OPPOSITION TO HOMOSEXUALITY

Christian News Today reports: "The Swedish government is moving toward prohibiting Christians from voicing biblical positions on issues. The Swedish Parliament has moved to within one step of **changing the nation's constitution** to ban speech or materials opposing homosexuality and any other alternate lifestyles. If the amendment becomes a reality, violators could be subject to prison sentences."

Folks, if we don't wake up and smell the spiritual coffee we are in deep danger. Keep an eye on those *Hate Crime Bills* in Congress – they may be issuing a warrant for your arrest, soon!

"God's sorest judgments, the ancients said, are like millstones; they grind very slowly, but they grind very fine. The thing I fear most for my country is gradual insensible dry rot and decay. But of one thing I am sure. The state that begins by sowing the seed of national neglect of God will sooner, or later, reap a national disaster and national ruin."

– JC RYLE

- CHAPTER 10-
CLOUDS OF JUDGMENT ON THE HORIZON

"The wicked shall be turned into hell,

and all the nations that forget God."

-Psalms 9:17

As we have thus far considered, this nation was founded upon biblical principles, and there are many who believe that this nation was founded to be a gospel "lighthouse" for the world. Like Israel of old, God had a divine purpose for this nation, and intended for this nation to be a fruitful vineyard for the good of the world and the glory of God. Unfortunately, instead of bringing forth fruit that remains (John 15:1-8), as a nation we have produced *"wild grapes"* (Isaiah 5:2 & 4). If the Word of God is true, any nation that turns its back on God will have to be sure to see the clouds of God's judgment on the horizon!

We are reminded in the Holy Writ that God's "blessing and cursing" are the consequences of our choices. There is no denying the fact that as a nation we have made the foolish choice, and because of it will reap the fatal consequences.

Deuteronomy 30:19, I call heaven and earth to record this day against you, that I have set before you life and death, blessing and cursing: therefore choose life, that both thou and thy seed may live.

In 2002, America is a sick and snarled network of everything that is a stench in the nostrils of a righteous and a holy God. As a nation, we love dishonesty and practice deceit, we love immorality rather than integrity, and our lives have become devoid of divine meaning. Our present moral condition is reminiscent of the Roman Empire at the time of her fall and France at the time of its Revolution.

Beyond a doubt, *"From the sole of the foot even unto the head there is no soundness"* (Isaiah 1:6a) in America today. The truth of God's Word *"is fallen in the street, and equity cannot enter"* (Isaiah 59:14). Like Israel of old, our *"wounds and bruises, and putrefying sores ... have not been closed, neither bound up, neither mollified with ointment"* (Isaiah 1:6b). Spiritually our *"country is desolate [and our] cities are burned with fire"* (Isaiah 1:7). This fire, of course, has been kindled from the very pit of hell.

The evil seeds of destruction that we have sown into the hearts of our citizenry are bringing forth a hellish harvest, and we will have "hell" to pay for it. God's universal principle of "sowing and reaping" (Galatians 6:7) has been set in motion as we have *"sown to the flesh."* As one author declared:

> God has been removed from the halls of our government buildings, our nation's classrooms, and most of our churches. The Constitution, though paid lip service to by those in authority, has been scrapped. And most people have been induced/seduced into accepting the diabolically obscene humanist dogma that they evolved from slime. ***That the United States is headed for judgment day is beyond dispute. God is not mocked. What we have sown, that we will surely reap!***[343]

Founding Father George Mason, while he was a Virginia delegate at the Constitutional Convention, said, "As nations cannot be rewarded or punished in the next world, they must be in this. By an inevitable chain of causes and effects, Providence punishes national sins by national calamities."[344] Our second president, Thomas Jefferson, asked "Can the liberties of a nation be thought secure when we have removed their only firm basis, a conviction in the minds of the people that these liberties are the gift from God?"

In 1954, Chief Justice Earl Warren said, "I like to believe we are living today in the spirit of the Christian religion. I like also to believe that as long as we do so, no great harm can come to our country." Another said, "America is running on the momentum of a godly heritage and when the momentum is spent, God help us!" It would appear that our "momentum is spent," and if that is the case, only God can help us.

Judgment is inevitable; the only question that remains to be answered is how soon we hit the wall of national destruction under the hand of an angry God, and at what speed will we hit the wall. God always warns a nation before judgment. God is longsuffering, merciful and extremely slow to anger. Nevertheless, there is a point in time when God's patience runs out and His punishment for sin kicks in. Has America crossed God's deadline? Is it possible that we are presently, and have been for sometime, under the hand of God's judgment? Someone once wrote:

> The foundations of present day America are no longer solid rocks cemented in its Christian heritage: They have become brittle clay crumbling under the judgment of God.

After we kicked God out of the government-run school system, it wasn't long before the void became apparent. Vice, vulgarity and violence became everyday activities, not only on the school campuses, but also in the community. As our nation tolerated the abominable sin of homosexuality as an "alternative life-style," as well as sexual promiscuity among heterosexuals, we have reaped the consequences of sexually transmitted diseases. After legalizing "murder," also known by the pagans as abortion, our nation has seen violence in our country skyrocket.

After many years of almost uninterrupted and unprecedented prosperity and divine protection, it would appear that not only have we as a nation forgotten God, but also I believe that God has removed from America His hand of blessing. It was the blessing of God that prospered, protected and preserved this nation for so long and actually "exalted" us above all others. I believe that over the past fifty or sixty years our nation has lost her innocence, her integrity, and in the past decade, we have lost our invincibility. God has removed the hedge of protection from our nation. (See Isaiah 5:1-7; Ecclesiastes 10:7 & Job 1:10.)

The law of sowing and reaping is immutable. The destruction of a nation is the eventual result of a nation that has turned its back on God. Back in 1893, a preacher named J.C. Ryle declared that:

> God's sorest judgments, the ancients said, are like millstones; they grind very slowly, but they grind very fine. The thing I fear most for my country is gradual insensible dry rot and decay. But of one thing I am sure. The state that begins by sowing the seed of national neglect of God will sooner, or later, reap a national disaster and national ruin.

As Bible-believing Christians, we must recognize the spiritual side of every political and economic issue. We must look into the Word of God, which rules in the affairs of mankind, and look for the reason that God could possibly "permit" what we are witnessing in our nation today. God's message to Israel can and should be applied to America today.

Deuteronomy 28:1-2, 20, 49 & 52, And it shall come to pass, if thou shalt hearken diligently unto the voice of the LORD thy God, to observe and to do all his commandments which I command thee this day, that the LORD thy God will set thee on high above all nations of the earth: And all these blessings shall come on thee, and overtake thee, if thou shalt hearken unto the voice of the LORD thy God.... The LORD shall send upon thee cursing, vexation, and rebuke, in all that thou settest thine hand unto for to do, until thou be destroyed, and until thou perish quickly; because of the wickedness of thy doings, whereby thou hast forsaken me.... The LORD shall bring a nation against thee from far, from the end of the earth, as swift as the eagle flieth; a nation whose tongue thou shalt not understand.... And he shall besiege thee in all thy gates, until thy high and fenced walls come down, wherein thou trustedst, throughout all thy land: and he shall besiege thee in all thy gates throughout all thy land, which the LORD thy God hath given thee.

If the above verses don't sound like America, I don't know what does. The backdrop of world history is sprinkled with the ruins of nations that once stood exalted for all to behold, who allowed self-indulgence from within to bring them to destruction. Has God been blind to the vice of our "blessed" nation? Can and will God continue to bless us in the midst of our spiritual ignorance, indifference, idolatry and immorality? God's Word repeatedly warns that, without repentance, judgment is inevitable. In **Proverbs 34:14** the proverbial writer inspired of God warns us:

"Righteousness exalteth a nation; but sin is a reproach to any people."

Is it possible that the long dark shadow of God's judgment is already covering our land? The prophets Isaiah and Jeremiah were alive when Israel and Judah were destroyed. These prophets along with others were used by God to warn His people of the judgment to come. As you well know, God's people refused to receive the Word and repent from their sin and the result was death, destruction and for many, deliverance into bondage. When the people of God would not recognize the tragedies as the hand of God, Jeremiah said: *"My people know not the judgment of the Lord"* (**Jeremiah 8:7**)

Someone once said, "If free men lost their freedom, it was because they were too apathetic to take note while the precious waters of God-given freedom slipped, drop by drop, down the drain." Could it be possible that we have been "hoodwinked" into believing that everything is all right?

Many of us today are like the people of God in Jeremiah's day. Both of our nations had a godly heritage. Both Israel of old and America today turned their backs on God and went into gross immorality and idolatry while maintaining a religious appearance. Like Israel, we have practiced child killing, and have tolerated homosexuality. As a nation we have been warned of the upcoming judgment, and we have refused to listen.

A statement made by the great preacher, Jonathan Edwards, rings truer in America today than in his day. Edwards said, God is "an angry God without any promise or obligation at all."[345] As one great Methodist evangelist said, "How right Edwards was! What obligations has God to a people like us whose aggregate sin as a nation in one day is more than the sin of Sodom and her sister city, Gomorrah, in one year?"[346]

How can we possibly expect anything less than the "hand of judgment" to come upon this nation after our continual rejection of His Word and refusal to repent of the abominations that take place daily in America. There is little doubt, actually no doubt at all, that the "only reason we are not smoking in the fire wrath of a holy God" is because of His mercy. Is God obliged to bless America when she refuses to bless Him? I think not!

An old Methodist preacher was right by saying, "If God puts the millstone of our sin around the neck of this generation and casts us into the nethermost depths of hell, that would be our just desert."[347] Historian Will Durant has rightly said, "We have reached our zenith, and are beginning to crumble and share with Second Century Rome great wealth, great freedom, loss of religious faith, and have overextended ourselves in the world with wide avenues of commitment."

The people of God are so indifferent today to reaching the lost with the gospel of Jesus Christ and making a real difference in our communities, first, and then our country. As the old preacher said, "We are chronically lazy and so callously indifferent! As lax, loose, lustful, and lazy Laodiceans, we are challenging God to spew us out of His mouth. God pity us or smite us!"[348]

More and more each day, we find the American dream being transformed into the American nightmare. A corporation executive warned against over-optimism with these words: "We should not be misled by the appearance of a light at the end of the tunnel. It is probably an oncoming train."[349]

SEPTEMBER 11: A FINAL 9-1-1 CALL FROM GOD?

Though our nation had weathered many disasters, including other terrorist attacks in her 225-year history, nothing had ever motivated such a sensation of catastrophe before, the feeling that the entire nation was at the mercy of a nameless and faceless threat. For our generation, Tuesday, September 11, was surely a day that will go down in infamy. In the words of one author, "The world as we know it ended Tuesday, September 11, 2001. It was a day of unspeakable terror that will be burned in the hearts and minds of all Americans forever."[350]

As one mall manager told a Milwaukee reporter, "You just feel like the country has been violated in a manner that those of our generation can't fathom." One lady interviewed by a *Gazette-Times* reporter said, "It's taken a while to sink in, I'm probably like everyone else. I have this sick feeling in my stomach ... it changes the way we look at ourselves. *It's just too big to comprehend.*" The *Daily Oklahoman* quoted a Susan Hunt who said, " I don't know if I am crying for me or crying for the nation ... it brings back those old horrifying feelings of the lack of security." Of course, our fears have continued even to this day!

Indeed, as a result of what many world leaders described as an *act of war*, the greatest nation in the history of mankind came to a virtual standstill. Our entire nation was jolted by the tragic events of September 11. Americans sought, and are still seeking, for answers as they paused in front of their television sets, listened to their radios, read their daily papers, and even sought refuge in churches and synagogues throughout our nation. And, of course, that didn't last for long!

The most powerful man in the world, our own president, and his family were quickly taken away for their own safety. For the first time in our nation's history, every airport was closed, the New York Stock Exchange suspended trading, Disneyland and Disney World, along with other places and sources of entertainment, were evacuated or canceled as safety measures.

The most horrific day in the history of our nation began when a passenger plane, en route to Los Angeles, hijacked by Islamic radicals, was transformed into a "missile of death and

186

destruction." This "missile" was purposely flown into the New York City World Trade Center at 8:45 a.m. EST. In less than a half an hour, a second hijacked jetliner was used as an instrument of destruction slamming into the towers resulting in the total destruction. Slamming into the Twin Towers, the symbol of *America's economic might,* another hijacked plane rammed into the Pentagon, the symbol of *America's military might.* The two crashes caused the death of nearly 4,000 people.

A fourth jetliner was hijacked, but according to all reports, brave passengers who refused to die without a fight, overpowered the hijackers. Their heroism saved countless lives in Washington D.C., in what most authorities claim would have been an attack on the White House or the U.S. Capitol.

As one author put it, "there was no denying the enormity of what had happened."[351] Headlines from the major magazines clearly stated, *The Day That Changed America, God Bless America,*[352] *September 11, 2001 The Day That Shook America,*[353] and then there were magazines such as *Time,* left speechless, who simply put a picture on the cover. This day of national tragedy, in the words of one author, was "far worse than Pearl Harbor."[354]

In the course of the grief, this terrible tragedy raised a multitude of troublesome questions. How could this nation, one that spends tens of billions annually on intelligence gathering, be caught so unprepared, and especially in the face of what had been a plan that took years to bring to fruition? How could four commercial jetliners be hijacked almost simultaneously?

How could the Pentagon, the center of our military leadership, be so easily overcome by a commercial jetliner, forty minutes after the initial attack in New York City? The terrorist attacks on the World Trade Center in New York and the Pentagon in Washington D.C., along with the massive toll in lost lives, property damage, emotional trauma, and economic disruption have shaken the nation at its very foundations. As one author stated, "Our once naïve perception of national invulnerability has been shattered. From coast-to-coast, and border-to-border, doubts, fears, and uncertainties are everywhere present. Is it possible that America will never be the same again?"[355] Is it possible that our nation is, as this same author put it, is moving "ever-closer to the precipice leading to a national disaster?"[356]

Our generation has heard the Word of God proclaimed, but as a nation we have foolishly rejected the truth of God's Word, and therefore, we have been witnesses to a brewing storm that will eventually engulf our nation. God declares, "Because thou hast rejected knowledge, I will also reject thee ... seeing thou hast forgotten the law of thy God, I will also reject thee." (Hosea 4:6)

The winds of apathy, apostasy and anarchy have been blowing across this great land for many years now, and I believe that September 11, 2001, will be a day of infamy that will always be known as the beginning of the end of this once great nation. The result of years of apathy, apostasy, and anarchy will no doubt be years of an adversity that we as a nation have never had to experience because God's hand of blessing was upon us. As Britain's General, Micheal Rose, put it, "It demonstrates that there's no such thing as total security."

SEPTEMBER 11 – WHY?

Many will tell us that September 11 "happened because we have an open border policy that makes it impossible to tell who is in our country and for what reason."[357] And humanly speaking there is merit to this answer. But far more important and dangerous than our physical geographical borders being opened for all to enter is the fact that we have opened our "spiritual borders" to every form of vice known to mankind. Author Dinesh D'Souza was right on target when he noted,

> The most serious charge against America is not that it is an oppressive society, or one that denies freedom and opportunity to minorities. It is the charge that America is an immoral society.

Others have responded to this question by saying, "It happened because our enemies believe America lacks the will to win." Concerning this, one author reminds us:

> We committed our military forces to Vietnam for twelve years and were not able, even with our massive military resources, to defeat a nation the size of Vermont. Simply stated, America's politicians were not committed to victory.[358]

Much of the turmoil, tragedy and tyranny reigning in our nation today are the result of our unwillingness to fight and fight to win. Douglas MacArthur, the great World War II general, said it well when he stood before a joint session of Congress after being relieved of command in Korea. "In war," MacArthur said, "there is no substitute for victory."[359] Far more detrimental to America's present situation is our lack of desire to win our spiritual battles.

Ever since 9/11, attentive Americans have been asking the question, sometimes in sophisticated ways, but at other times in very simple ways. Did the tragedy on 9/11 occur because America is good, or because America has become a disgracefully godless nation?" Of course, only God's Word can provide an appropriate answer to a very sensitive question. And any one individual who would attempt to be the final and authoritative voice would have to be "both arrogant and presumptuous." Romans 11 asks, *"For who hath known the mind of the Lord?"*

As one author wrote, "The flip side of the question keeps perplexing thoughtful people. It's not a question of whether we were as evil as the terrorists were; almost everyone assumes that we're not. It's just the nagging thought that one way or another; God was rattling our chain and reminding us that our own cavalierly secular inattention to Him may also carry a price. And if that indeed is the case – if it's the case that God is actually saying something – then embarrassing as it may to be to admit it, shouldn't we pay Him some attention? For even if our shortcomings are relatively minor (as we suppose ours to be), doesn't the God of the whole universe nonetheless hold the prerogative of reminding us – who have enjoyed His blessings so extravagantly – that we owe Him at least something."[360]

There are those who object that the "God of their definition would ... resort to such an overstatement while issuing such a reminder."[361] This same author asks an intriguing question: "Does God, in such circumstances, have the right and the ability to say anything at all to us? Can we recognize that right and ability independently of what we think about the evil of the enemy."[362]

In the end, if we can finally say yes to this fundamental question, another vital issue is exposed. That issue is our pride. Once we acknowledge that an external word from God is an appropriate part of both our personal and national experience, then we have been humbled.

"We will not fail," were the words of President George Bush concerning our "war against terrorism." But as Bible-believing Christians, we must not be deceived into thinking that because we are the most prosperous and powerful nation in the world – we will not fail. The question that must be asked and answered in the light of God's words is very simple, but extremely important. Is God willing to allow us to continue as the world's most prosperous, powerful and prestigious nation?

There can be little doubt that trying days are ahead for the United States of America. It is inevitable that we pay for our lawlessness and lewdness, and our rampant rebellion against all that is true and holy. It's not a matter of *if;* it is simply a matter of *when.* As one author is quick to remind us, "Rebellious man hasn't broken the laws – social, educational, financial etc. – written eternally in the heavens. He has just violated them. Those laws are still in full force and affect. They are perfect. They are immutable. They work. They will inevitably break and crush underfoot all who violate them – from the greatest to the least of us. The wheels of justice turn slowly but relentlessly." God help us!

Historians are quick to remind us that right through history there have been numerous "most powerful" nations and empires, but all had, in time, become corrupt, calloused and, in due time, collapsed. *Could America be next?*

- CHAPTER 11 -

IT'S TIME TO FIGHT

"Thou therefore, my son, be strong in the grace that is in Christ Jesus. ... Thou therefore endure hardness, as a good soldier of Jesus Christ. ... I have fought a good fight, I have finished my course, I have kept the faith."

- II Timothy 2:1 & 3, 4:7

Amerrica, more than anything else, needs men and women who are *"strong in the grace that is in Christ Jesus,"* and who are willing to *"endure hardness, as a good soldier of Jesus Christ."* Our country needs a multitude of men and women who can truly say, with the apostle Paul, *"I have fought a good fight, I have finished my course, I have kept the faith."*

As we are reminded in Ezekiel 9:4, America desperately needs *"men that sigh and that cry for all the abominations that be done in the midst thereof."* God knows where we would be today if it hadn't been for a very small "remnant" of men and women in this nation who have prayed and worked for America's deliverance.

Isaiah 1:9, "Except the Lord of hosts had left us a very small remnant, we should have been as Sodom, and we should have been like unto Gomorrah."

This book has been a call for those who are willing to "fight the good fight of faith," and beat back the attempts of the enemies of Christ and His cross. One author rightly claimed, "Our founding fathers beat back the attempts of the secularizers

193

200 years ago. If they were living today, I know whose side they would champion."[363]

Will we heed the warning of those who have come before us? Will we do our part in saving America, or will we sit back and watch as our freedoms dissipate with each passing day? Someone has rightly said, "If free men lost their freedom, it was because they were too apathetic to take note while the precious waters of God-given freedom slipped, drop by drop, down the drain."[364]

It has been said, "If America ever dies it will be because she forgot how to live." If I may do so, I would like to add to that statement the following words, "Not only did America forget how to live, but she has also forgotten how to fight." If America is worth living in, she is worth fighting for.

God is looking for men, women and young people filled with courage from above who will "stand in the gap," and make a real difference in their community. We need churches and pastors that will preach the Word, reach the lost, and train up the saved to be "vessels meet for the Master's use," and soldiers ready to not only fight, but also fight to win! We need to "arise and be doing," put our "hands to the plow," and get on with the job at hand – saving the lost and saving America!

> **Ezekiel 22:30-31,** *"And I sought for a man among them, that should make up the hedge, and stand in the gap before Me for the land, that I should not destroy it: but I found none."*

We are all called to be soldiers of Christ, whether we like it or not, and to stand for truth and righteousness in America. If we are going to make an impact, it will "require greater commitment and sacrifice in the days ahead." It is high time we lay aside our petty differences, sacrifice some of our comforts, draw the Sword of the Lord, God's Holy Word, and get out to the front lines of the battlefield!

Where is the heart of the warrior? Where is the will to war? Where are the men and the women who will rise up empowered by the Spirit of God, led by the Word of God, motivated by the love of God, and a love for our country, and angered by what has, and is transpiring in this once great country? Concerning a "righteous indignation," one author has stated:

> Many Americans [are] enraged, but feel they must obey ... As long as Americans believe that their government is acting constitutionally, they will obey ... by definition, and conservatives are not rebels. But neither were the founding fathers until they were pushed to the wall.[365]

We need some men and women who feel "pushed to the wall." Folks, we had better accept the fact that we are stuck in a difficult situation. In the words of Dr. Sam Francis, "The first thing we have to learn about fighting and winning a culture war, is that we are not fighting to 'conserve' something, we are fighting to overthrow something."[366] Francis continues with this thought by writing:

> We must understand clearly and firmly that the dominant authorities in ... the major foundations, the media, the schools, the universities, and most of the system of organized culture, including the arts and entertainment – not only do nothing to conserve what most of us regard as our traditional way of life, but actually seek its destruction or are indifferent to its survival. If our culture is going to be conserved, then we need to dethrone the dominant authorities that threaten it.[367]

WE NEED A REBIRTH OF BRAVERY AND COURAGE

"Be strong and of a good courage ... Only be thou strong and very courageous, that thou mayest observe to do according to all the law, which Moses my servant commanded thee: turn not from it to the right hand or to the left, that thou mayest prosper whithersover thou goest." Joshua 1:6a-7

Our nation is sickly, desperately sick, and we are in dire need of the "healing power" of the Great Physician to touch and heal our land. America has come to a place where, if something doesn't happen soon, and if the insanity continues, it's over! Lord knows we need a revival in the land. If a revival doesn't come soon, it's over! Robert Bork once wrote: "I am not a religious man, but America is now in moral anarchy. I do not believe it can even survive without a sweeping spiritual revival."

> **2 Chronicles 7:14,** *If My people, which are called by My name, shall humble themselves, and pray, and seek My face, and turn from their wicked ways; then will I hear from heaven, and will forgive their sin, and will heal their land.*

In the words of John Stormer, "America needs a rebirth of the political and spiritual principles which were the 'nerves' and 'blood' of the Republic for almost 200 years."[368] As we all well know, if that is going to happen, God will have to raise up men who are dedicated to the political, social and spiritual principles that laid the foundation of this nation. Addressing the slavery issue in poem, James Russell Lowell said:

Once to every man and nation

Comes the moment to decide,

In the strife of truth with falsehood,

For the good or evil side,

Then it is the brave, who chooses,

While the coward stands aside,

'Til the multitude makes virtue

Of the faith they had denied...

Though the cause of evil prosper,

Yet 'tis truth alone is strong;

... Standeth God within the shadow,

Keeping watch above His own.[369]

We are living in the midst of a great conflict between truth and falsehood. May God raise up, in our churches and throughout our country, men and women who are bravely devoted to join in the battle on the side of truth.

"PULPITS AFLAME WITH RIGHTEOUSNESS"

"Cry aloud, spare not, lift up thy voice like a trumpet, and shew my people their transgression, and the house of Jacob their sins." – Isaiah 58:1

When Alexis de Tocqueville remarked that in the churches of America he "heard the pulpits aflame with righteousness," and he recognized that these pulpits and this type of preaching were the secret and source of America's "genius and power," he was simply reminding us that there is tremendous power in the pulpit of an anointed man of God. Lord knows, we need men who will *"Cry aloud, spare not, lift up [their] voice like a trumpet;"* and we need men who will *"Preach the Word; be instant in season, out of season; reprove, rebuke, exhort with all longsuffering and doctrine"* (II Timothy 4:2).

Unfortunately, too many of our pulpits are silent today. Compromise, comfort and complacency are the trademarks of the hour. God knows we need some "liberated" men who will preach the Word of God, endued by the Spirit of God, to the people of God. John Greenleaf Whittier once asked, "Where's the manly spirit of the truehearted and unshackled gone?"

God knows we need some men in the pulpit of our churches who will stand up and *"blow the trumpet in Zion"* (Joel 2:1), calling on the troops of God to battle. Would to God that we would see and hear more men today proclaiming boldly the principles and precepts of God's Holy Word. When the first dynasty was falling into ruins, on an Egyptian tomb someone inscribed the words, "And no one is angry enough to speak out."[370] God knows we need some men to become "angry enough to speak out." Martin Luther, the father of the Protestant Reformation, was a fighter. Notice his words:

> I never work better than when I am inspired of anger; when I am angry, I can write, pray, preach well, for then my whole temperament is quickened, my understanding sharpened, and my mundane vexations and temptations depart.

This same Luther when finding himself between a rock and a hard place because of his biblical convictions said, "Here I stand; I can do no other." Athanasius, champion of the complete deity of Christ against the Arians who denied it, was told, "The whole world is against you." His reply was, "Then I am against the whole world." Lord, give us men with this same spirit of Luther and Athanasius.

America is at War, and we need some prophets on the frontlines of the battle. Prophets are fearless men who are willing to denounce the sins of their day. Prophets of God call men away from idols back to God. A true prophet is concerned about the moral and political corruption of the nation, but the fact that the people were worshipping idols is his greatest concern. Prophets of the Most High constantly remind the people that Jehovah is the only true God, and that Christ is the only way. Prophets were statesmen of the highest order. God, raise up some prophets in our churches and our Christian schools!

The prophets were unpopular in their day, for they dealt with the moral and religious conditions of the hour! Generally the state was bad. Prophets were sent when the nation was out of step with God – when they were walking in disobedience. The words which the prophets used to rebuke or exhort the people were very pointed. We need some men who have within their breast the same spirit that inspired the prophets of old.

We need men who, like the great apostle Paul, will be "stirred" within by the idolatry, indifference and immorality that have become commonplace here in America.

*Acts 17:16, "Now while Paul waited for them at Athens, **his spirit was stirred in him**, when he saw the city wholly given to idolatry."*

We need men who are "stirred up" today. Concerning his preaching, Whitfield once said, "I set myself on fire and people come to watch me burn." Oh, Lord, set our souls on fire today!

The apostle Paul also said, *"I am pure from the blood of all men"* (Acts 20:26). The apostle Paul understood that we are all accountable for "warning" and "winning" people by proclaiming the Word of God in the sphere of our influence; if we choose not to do so, the blood of many stains our hands.

Ezekiel 3:17-18, "Son of man, I have made thee a watchman unto the house of Israel: therefore hear the word at my mouth, and give them warning from Me. When I say unto the wicked, Thou shalt surely die;

and thou givest him not warning, nor speakest to warn the wicked from his wicked way, to save his life ... his blood will I require at thine hand."

Ezekiel 33:7-9, *"So thou, O son of man, I have set thee a watchman unto the house of Israel; therefore thou shalt hear the word at My mouth, and warn them from Me. When I say unto the wicked, O wicked man, thou shalt surely die; if thou dost not speak to warn the wicked from his way, that wicked man shall die in his iniquity; but his blood will I require at thine hand."*

How could Paul have the calm assurance to make such a bold statement? Paul's confidence arose from the fact that he "kept back nothing" from the people, preaching all the "counsel of God" to them.

Acts 20:20 & 27, *"And how I kept back nothing that was profitable unto you, but have shewed you, and have taught you publicly, and from house to house ... For I have not shunned to declare unto you all the counsel of God."*

The people of God are going to have to become proactive and get in the *battle for the future of our nation.* Someone has rightly said, "Men are blind – we must lead them. Men are bound – we must free them. Sinful men are spiritually diseased – we must heal them. Godless men are dead – we must raise them from the dead by the Holy Spirit's power."

It is time we make our voice be heard, not only within the four walls of our church auditorium, but from also house-to-house and in the House (Congress). John Witherspoon once said:

He is the best friend of American liberty who is the most sincere and active in the promoting true and undefiled religion and who sets himself with the greatest firmness to bear down on profanity and immorality of every kind.[371]

The great evangelist Charles Finney once declared:

> The church must take right ground in regards to politics.... The time has come for Christians to vote for honest men, and take consistent ground in politics or the Lord will curse them...

> God cannot sustain this free and blessed country, which we love and pray for, unless the Church will take right ground. Politics are a part of a religion in such country as this, and Christians must do their duty to their country as a part of their duty to God...

> God will bless or curse this nation according to the course Christians take in politics.[372]

SILENT PULPITS

In the 1980s, Don Wildmon, wrote an excellent column entitled, "300,000 Silent Pulpits" that is definitely worth sharing:

> Today, 4,000 precious innocent lives of unborn babies were snuffed out....

> And 300,000 pulpits are silent....

> The networks make a mockery of Christians, the Christian faith and Christian values with nearly every show they air. Greed, materialism, violence, sexual immorality are standard fare. Program after program, movie after movie contains anti-Christian episodes and plots. News articles condescendingly refer to the "fundamentalist, right-wing Christian." Those who speak out for the sacredness of life are branded as extremists.

> And 300,000 pulpits are silent....

> Teenage suicide is higher than it's ever been... Christian morality cannot be taught in schools but atheistic immorality can....

> And 300,000 pulpits are silent....

Rape has increased 700 percent in the last fifty years, and that takes into consideration the population growth....

And 300,000 pulpits are silent....

Rock music fills the airwaves and our children's minds with music, which legitimizes rape, murder, forced sex, sadomasochism, adultery, satanic worship, etc...

And 300,000 pulpits are silent....

A majority of the states now have lotteries. We have eliminated the crime by making it legal and putting it under the control of the state.

And 300,000 pulpits are silent....

What important matters are being dealt with in our churches? The church bulletin says there will be a meeting to plan a church-wide supper. We are raising money to put in a new floor cover on the kitchen. (The old one doesn't match the new stove and refrigerator.) The sermon subject last week was "How to Have a Positive Attitude." We are organizing a softball team.

At a meeting of church officials a program was announced to recruit new members. We need the program because we are losing membership. The new program was worked out by some of the very top professionals, people who have had success in gaining new members for the Lions Club, the Citivan Club and other organizations. We really need professionals to do the job

Sometimes blasphemy comes unnoticed.[373]

As Dr. Kennedy wrote, "Thankfully, not all 300,000 pulpits are silent!" But, unfortunately, most are. Austin Sorenson in his book *Is America Committing Suicide?* asks a very probing question, "Have we lost our will to live? Do we no longer possess the instinct of self-preservation?"[374]

IT'S TIME TO CHOOSE

"Multitudes, multitudes in the valley of decision: for the day of the Lord is near in the valley of decision." – Joel 3:14

According to the Scriptures, *"The Lord is **far** from the wicked ... "* (Proverbs 15:29). As one saint of old noted, "We are as close to Jesus as we want to be." Like Joshua of old, we need to draw a line in the sand and "choose" today whom we will serve, not only as individual Christians, but our churches also need to make the choice, as does our country.

The hour has come, the midnight hour is drawing nearer, we must recognize that we are *"in the valley of decision,"* and the decisions we make today will determine the destiny our country has tomorrow. Our choices will produce consequences, but we must not fear and we must not delay. It is time to choose!

It was the Baron Opperheim who once said, "To every people there comes one terrible and inevitable final hour, when it must choose between those things by which men live, or those things by which they die." Another said, "Freedom is not free but must be earned anew by each succeeding generation." We can no longer live on the merits or the "momentum" of the past and previous generations. Thank God for those who have blazed the trail of freedom and fruitfulness for America, but it is now our turn to take the baton and *"run the race that is set before us"* (Hebrews 12:1).

The British statesmen, Edmund Burke once rightly said, "All that is necessary for evil to triumph is for good men to sit back and do nothing." An unknown author once wrote, "The price that good people pay for their apathy and indifference in public affairs is that they are ruled by evil men." On another occasion, Burke said, "People never give up their liberty except under some delusion." Far too many of God's people have been deceived into disobedience. Our disobedience is evident by our silence.

William Arthur Ward once wrote these words: "When we should speak out against evil, our silent assent is self-damaging, as destructive and as cowardly as verbal consent." One unknown author said it well, "Men and women become accomplices to those evils they fail to oppose." Peter Muhlenberg, a preacher turned patriot during our War for Independence, said, "There is a time to preach and a time to fight, and that time has come." May the Spirit of God raise up some men who are willing to fight.

Liberty is defined as rights with responsibilities. Of course, on the other hand, license is defined as rights with no responsibilities. If America is going to remain the "Land of the Free, and the Home of the Brave," we are going to have to be willing to pay the price for freedom. As someone has rightly said, "Liberty may be sweet, but it isn't cheap." Another has written:

> To be born a free man is an accident;
>
> To live a free man is a responsibility;
>
> To die a free man is an obligation.

Each and every Christian in this nation is "obligated" to live in such a way to ensure that this nation remains free. The words of Winston Churchill ring true today, truer than the day in which they were spoken:

> If you will not fight for the right when you can easily win without bloodshed, if you will not fight when your victory will be sure, and not too costly. You may come to the moment when you will have to fight with all odds against you, and only a perilous chance of survival. Because there is a worse case, you may have to fight

when there will be no hope for survival, for it will be better to perish than to live as slaves.

In October of 1956 in Hungary, fearless freedom fighters, standing against the Communist Russians, and understanding the "obligation of all free men to oppose slavery in every form," called for the help of other freedom-loving people around the world. As one of the last acts of the uprising against the Russians, a group of freedom-fighters got control of a radio station and broadcast this message to the rest of the world:

> People of the World ...help us!
>
> People of Europe, whom we once defended against the attacks of the Asiatic barbarians, listen now to the alarm bells ring. People of the civilized world, in the name of liberty and solidarity, we are asking for you to help.
>
> The light vanishes. The shadows grow darker hour by hour. Listen to our cry. God be with you and with us.[375]

And with that, the radio station went off the air. The plea for help was unheard and unheeded. The Russians were the only ones listening, and they shut the station off the air. The Russians succeeded in suppressing the uprising of the freedom fighters. Like the radio call, this book is a call from just one of many "freedom-fighters" in America today – will the call go unheard?

We have to wake up and recognize, if America is going to be salvaged, we must rise up with the light of God's Word – the "torch of truth," and spread it throughout the land, as revolutionaries, not conservatives. Someone has rightly written:

> No one came to the rescue.
>
> But the light does not need to vanish.
>
> You now have the torch of truth.
>
> How much light you spread is up to you. [376]

Someone once rightly declared, "Lest we despair, recall from both biblical and secular history that the character of a nation is not necessarily determined by the majority of its people – a deeply committed minority is quite sufficient. If God spared an entire nation because of the dedication of one woman named Esther, if He spared multitudes because of the prayers of one man named Moses, if God would have spared Sodom for ten righteous people in Sodom, then will not the Almighty spare this great nation because of the leavening influence of some truly converted people."

This is the need of the hour, a minority of people who will rise to the occasion and become involved in the battle for the future of our nation. Dr. Carl F. H. Henry, in the early 70s, then editing *Christianity Today*, posed the following question to some leading Christian thinkers: "Sighting the final third of the Twentieth-Century, what do you think it offers the church?" One of the Christian leaders replied with these words:

"By the year 2000, Christians will be a conscious minority surrounded by a militant paganism."

His words were prophetic! We are "a conscious minority," and we are definitely "surrounded by a militant paganism," and our only hope for survival is to proclaim the truth of God's Word to a lost and dying generation. We need some men who will "preach as never sure to preach again, and as a dying man to dying men." The truth of God's Word is the most powerful weapon that we have, and we must deploy it with wisdom, in love, but we must deploy it and now! If we do not do so, we may not "die as free men."

AMERICA THE BEAUTIFUL

(REVISED EDITION)

America the Beautiful, or so you used to be.

Land of the pilgrims' pride; I'm glad they'll never see.

Babies piled in dumpsters, Abortion on demand,

Oh, sweet land of liberty, your house in on the sand.

Our children wander aimlessly   poisoned by cocaine,

Choosing to indulge their lusts, when God has said abstain.

From sea to shining sea, our nation turns away

From teaching of God's love and a need to always pray.

So many worldly preachers tell lies about our Rock,

Saying God is going broke so they can fleece the flock.

We've kept God in our temples, how callous we have grown.

When earth is but His footstool, and Heaven is His throne.

We've voted in a government that's rotting at the core,

Appointing Godless judges who throw reason out the door,

Too soft to place a killer in a well deserved tomb,

But brave enough to kill a baby before he leaves the womb.

You think that God's not angry, that our land's a moral slum?

How much longer will He wait before His judgment comes?

How are we to face our God, from Whom we cannot hide?

What then is left for us to do, but stem this evil tide?

If we who are His children, will humbly pray;

Seek His holy face and mend our evil way:

The God will hear from Heaven and forgive us of our sins,

He'll heal our sickly land and those who live within.

But, America the Beautiful, if you don't then you will see,

A sad but Holy God withdraw His hand from Thee.

- Cited in *MIDNIGHT MESSENGER*

SELECTED BIBLIOGRAPHIES

Adams, Robert M., *Decadent Societies*, North Point Press, 1983

Adams, O.R., As We Sodomize America, Winepress Publishing, 2001

Barton, David, *America: To Pray or not to Pray?* David Barton, 1988

Barton, David, *The Myth of Separation*, Wall Builders Press, 1992

Barton, David, *Original Intent: The Courts, the Constitution, & Religion*, WallBuilder Press, 1999

Beckwith, Francis J. and Koukl, Gregory, Relativism, Baker Book House, 2002

Bennett, William J., *The De-Valuing of America: The Fight for our Culture and our Children*, Touchstone 1992

Blumenfeld, Samuel L., *Is Public Education Necessary?*, The Devin-Adair Company, 1981

Boorstin, Daniel J., *The Americans: The Colonial Experience*, Random House, 1958

Brewer, David J., *The United States, A Christian Nation*, American Vision Inc., 1995

Buchanan, Patrick J., *The Death of the West*, St. Martin's Press, 2002

Codevilla, Angelo M., *The Character of Nations: How Politics Makes and Breaks Prosperity, Family, and Civility*, Basic Books 1997

Demar, Gary, *God and Government Vol. 1, 2, 3*, American Vision, 2001

Demar, Gary, *America's Christian History: The Untold Story*, American Vision, 1995

Dewey, John and others, *Humanist Manifestos I & II*, Promotheus Books, 1973

Eidsmoe, John, *Christianity and the Constitution: The Faith of Our Founding Fathers*, Baker Books, 2000

Esposito, Johnny, *Temples of Darkness*, Pacific Publications 2001

Feder, Don, *A Jewish Conservative Looks at Pagan America*, Huntington House Publishers, 1993

Federer, William J., *America's God and Country*, Fame Publishing, 1994

Ham, Ken and Morris, John and Morris, Henry and Wieland, Carl and Henry, Jonathan and Cuozzo, Jack, *When Christians Roamed the Earth: Is the Bible-Believing Church Headed for Extinction?*, Master Books, 2002

Himmelfarb, Gertrude, *One Nation, Two Cultures*, Vintage Books, 2001

Hirsen, James, L., *The Coming Global Collision: Global Law vs. U.S. Liberties*, Huntington House Publishers, 1999

Jeffrey, Grant R., *Final Warning: Economic Collapse and the Coming World Government*, Frontier Research Publications, Inc. 1995

Jeffrey, Grant R., *Prince of Darkness: Antichrist and the New World Order*, Frontier Research Publications, Inc., 1994

Johnson, Paul, *A History of the American People*, Harper Perennial, 1999

Kaestle, Carl F., *Pillars of the Republic*, Hill and Wang, 1983

Kennedy, James, Dr., *The Gates of Hell Shall Not Prevail: The Attack On Christianity And What You Need To Know To Combat It*, Thomas Nelson Publishers, 1996

Keyes, Alan, *Our Character, Our Future*, Zondervon Publishing, 1996

Kilpatrick, William, *Why Johnny Can't Tell Right from Wrong: Moral Illiteracy and the Case for Character Education*, Simon and Schuster 1992

King, David James, M.D., *Creating A Nation Under God, Rebuilding America with Biblical Principles*, Prescott Press, 2000

Lahaye, Tim, *Faith of Our Founding Fathers*, Wolgemuth and Hyatt Publishers, Inc., 1987

Lahaye, Tim, *Mind Siege: The Battle for Truth in the New Millenium*, World

Lapin, Rabbi Daniel, *America's Real War*, Multnomah Publishers, 1999

McAlvany, Don, *Storm Warning: The Coming Persecution of Christians and Traditionalists in America*, Hearthstone Publishers, 1999

McTernan, John, *God's Final Warning to America*, Hearthstone Publishers, 2001

Perloff, James, *The Shadows of Power: The Council on Foreign Relations and the American Decline*, Western Islands 2000

Rae, Debra, *ABCs of Globalism*, Huntington House Publishers, 1999

Ravenhill, Leonard, *Sodom Had No Bible*, Bethany House Publishers, 1983

Rushdoony, Rousas John, *This Independent Republic: Studies in the Nature and Meaning of American History*, Ross House Books, 2001

Shirer, William, L., *The Rise and Fall of the Third Reich*, Simon and Schuster, 1960

Sowell, Thomas, *Inside American Education: The Decline, The Deception, The Dogmas*, The Free Press, 1993

Still, William T., *New World Order: The Ancient Plan of Secret Societies*, Huntington House Publishers, 1990

Stringer, Phil, *The Transformation: America's Journey Toward the Darkness*, Landmark Baptist Press, 2001

Swanson, Kevin, *The Second Mayflower*, 1994

Thomas, Cal, *The Things that Matter Most*, Harper Collins Publishers, 1994

Tocqueville, Alexis de, *Democracy in America*, Bantam Books, 2000

ENDNOTES:

PREFACE

[1] Patrick Buchanan, *The Death of the West*, p. 179
[2] Kevin Swanson, *The Second Mayflower*, p. 8

INTRODUCTION

[3] Cited in *Is America Committing Suicide*, p. 107
[4] Alexis de Tocqueville, *Democracy in America*, p. 356
[5] Alexis de Tocqueville, *Democracy in America*, p. 356
[6] David A. Noebel, *The Battle for Truth*, p. viii
[7] Robert Bork, *Slouching Towards Gomorrah: Modern Liberalism and American Decline*, p. 6
[8] Cited in *America's Christian History*, p. 1
[9] Anthony Harrigan, *The New Anti-Civilization Chronicles*, June 2001, p. 44
[10] Cited in *Is America Committing Suicide ?*, p. 216

CHAPTER ONE – FRIENDS WE ARE AT WAR

[12] Cited in *America's God and Country*, p. 670
[13] Patrick J. Buchanan, *The Death of the West*, p. 6
[14] Cited in *The Death of the West*, p. 5

CHAPTER TWO – THE IMPORTANCE OF HISTORY

[15] Patrick J. Buchanan, *The Death of the West*, p. 5
[16] Cited in *It's Time to Remember America!*, p. vii
[17] Andrew Sandlin, Cited in *The Influence of Historic Christianity on Early America*, p. 1
[18] George Grant, *The Blood of the Moon*, p. 15
[19] George Grant, *The Blood of the Moon*, p. 15
[20] Cited in *The Death of the West*, p. 147
[21] Cited in *The Death of the West*, p. 147
[22] Cited in *The Death of the West*, p. 147
[23] Harold Rugg, *The Great Technology*, p. 32 & 271
[24] *Ibid.* 235
[25] *Ibid.* 237
[26] Report House Committee to Investigate Tax Exempt Foundations, 83rd Congress 1954, p. 150.
[27] *Ibid.*
[28] *Ibid.*
[29] *Ibid*, p. 155
[30] Tim LaHaye, *Faith of Our Founding Fathers*, p. 5

[31] *Ibid.*, p. 135

[32] Homer Duncan, *Secular Humanism*, p. 40

[33] Cited in *Erdman's Handbook to the History of Christianity*, p. 2

[34] Paul Johnson, *A History of the American People*, p. 3

CHAPTER THREE - OUR CHRISTIAN HERITAGE

[35] Daniel Lapin, *Americas Real War*, p. 95

[36] David J. Brewer, *The United States A Christian Nation*, p. 12

[37] David J. Brewer *The United States A Christian Nation*, p. 13-14

[38] David J. Brewer, *The United States A Christian Nation*, p. 40

[39] David J. Brewer, *The United States A Christian Nation*, p. 35

[40] David J. Brewer, *The United States A Christian Nation*, p. 35

[41] Cited in *What Hath God Wrought*, p. 46

[42] Cited in *What Hath God Wrought*, p. 46

[43] Archie P. Jones, *The Influence of Historic Christianity on Early America*, p. 28

[44] Des Griffin, *Descent into Slavery*, p. 6

[45] Archie P. Jones, *The Influence of Historic Christianity on Early America*, p. 29

[46] Cited in *The Influence of Historic Christianity on Early America*, p. 24

[47] Archie P. Jones, *The Influence of Historic Christianity on Early America*, p. 23-24

[48] Cited in *The Influence of Historic Christianity on Early America*, p. 24

[49] Sydney E. Ahlstrom, *A Religious History of the American People*, Vol. 1, p. 169

[50] Des Griffin, *Descent into Slavery*, p. 6

[51] Cited in *Faith of Our Founding Fathers*, p. 30

[52] Daniel Lapin, *America's Real War*, p. 95

[53] Daniel Lapin, *America's Real War*, p. 100

[54] Cited in *Political Sermons of the American Founding Era, 1730-1805*, Vol. 1

[55] Tim LaHaye, *Faith of our Founding Fathers*, p. 31

[56] Tim LaHaye, *Faith of our Founding Fathers*, p. 31

[57] Cited in *The Death of A Nation*, p. 130

[58] John Stormer, *The Death of A Nation*, p. 130

[59] John Stormer, *The Death of A Nation*, p. 131

[60] Cited in *God and Government*, Vol. 1, p. 1

[61] Patrick J. Buchanan, *The Death of the West*, p. 180-181

[62] Gary DeMarr, *America's Christian History*, p. 51-58

[63] Gary DeMarr, *America's Christian History*, p. 12

[64] Gary DeMarr, *America's Christian History*, p. 3

[65] Daniel Lapin, *America's Real War*, p. 35

[66] Associate Supreme Court Justice, David J. Brewer, *The United States A Christian Nation*, p. 44

[67] Cited in *America's Christian History: The Untold Story*, p. 2

[68] Gary DeMarr, *America's Christian History*, p. 11

[69] Gary DeMarr, *America's Christian History*, p. 12

[70] Gary DeMarr, *America's Christian History*, p. 2

[71] Gary DeMarr, *America's Christian History*, p. 11

[72] Gary DeMarr, *America's Christian History*, p. 3

[73] Cited in *Storming the Gates of Hell*, p. 6

[74] Cited in *Storming the Gates of Hell*, p. 7

[75] Cited in *Orations of American Orators*, Vol. I, p. 9

[76] David Barton, *The Spirit of the Revolution*, Video Presentation

[77] David Barton, *America's Godly Heritage*, Video Presentation

[78] David Barton, *America's Godly Heritage*, Video Presentation

[79] Cited in *Faith of Our Fathers*, p.40-41

[80] David Barton, *The Spirit of the Revolution*, Video Presentation

[81] David Barton, *The Spirit of the Revolution*, Video Presentation

[82] Cited in *Is America Committing Suicide?*, p. 105-106

[83] Cited in *Is America Committing Suicide?*, p. 107

[84] Cited in *God and Country*, p. 181

[85] *Newsweek*, July 6, 1970

[86] Daniel Marsh, *Unto the Generations*, p. 51

[87] Cited in *The Gates of Hell Shall Not Prevail*, p. 165

[88] Anthony Harrigan, *The New Anti-Civilization Chronicles*, June 2001, p. 44

[89] Jim Nelson Black, *When Nations Die*, p. 8

CHAPTER FOUR – THE FOUNDATIONS HAVE BEEN DESTROYED

[90] Carl Sommer, *Schools in Crisis: Training for Success or Failure*, p. 62

[91] Cited in *America's Christian History: The Untold Story*, p. 192

[92] Cited in *America's Christian History: The Untold Story*, p. 192

[93] Des Griffin, *Fourth Reich of the Rich*, p. 10

[94] Des Griffin, *Fourth Reich of the Rich*, p. 11

[95] Kevin Swanson, *The Second Mayflower*, p. 21-22

[96] Kevin Swanson, *The Second Mayflower*, p. 19

[97] Cal Thomas, *The Things That Matter Most*, p. 102

[98] Cal Thomas, *The Things That Matter Most*, p. 103

[99] Archibald Alexander, *Evidences of Authenticity, Inspiration and Canonical Authority of the Holy Scriptures*, p. 18

[100] Cal Thomas, *The Things That Matter Most*, p. 105-106

[101] Cal Thomas, *The Things That Matter Most*, p. 107

[102] *Ibid.*

[103] Bill Grady, *What Hath God Wrought*, p. XIV

ENDNOTES

[104] Ray Chamberlain, *Quotes and Quaint Stories of Great Americans*, p. 16

[105] Carl F. Kaestle, *Pillars of the Republic*, p.81

[106] Cited in *America's God and Country*, p. 669

[107] Gary DeMarr, *God and Government*, Vol. 2, p. 4-5

[108] "Issues 94" 19982 RAND Cooperation Study, cited by *Heritage Foundation*, 35

[109] Cited in *America's God and Country*, p. 678

[110] Robert Bork, *Slouching Towards Gomorrah: Modern Liberalism and American Decline*, Inside Flap

[111] Patrick J. Buchanan, *The Death of the West*, p. 179

[112] Tim LaHaye, *Faith of Our Founding Fathers*, p. 20

[113] Tim LaHaye, *Faith of Our Founding Fathers*, p. 22

[114] Tim LaHaye, *Faith of Our Founding Fathers*, p. 22

[115] Tim LaHaye, *Faith of Our Founding Fathers*, p. 22

[116] Tim LaHaye, *Faith of Our Founding Fathers*, p. 33

[117] Gary DeMar, *God and Government*, Vol. 1 p. 183

[118] Cited in *America's God and Country*, p. 296

[119] Cited in *America's God and Country*, p. 296

[120] Gary DeMar, *God and Government*, Vol. 1 p. 183

[121] Gary DeMar, *God and Government*, Vol. 1 p. 183

[122] Dr. James Kennedy, *The Gates of Hell Shall Not Prevail*, p. 67

[123] Cited in *The Collected Writings of James Henley Thornwell*, Vol. IV, p. 517

[124] Gary DeMar, *God and Government*, Vol. 1 p. 183

[125] Gary DeMar, *God and Government*, Vol. 1 p. 194

[126] *Letter to Samuel Miller*, January 23, 1808

[127] John W. Whitehead, *The Separation Illusion*, pp. 90-91

[128] Dr. James Kennedy, *The Gates of Hell Shall Not Prevail*, p. 142

[129] Cited in *The Gates of Hell Shall Not Prevail*, p. 142

[130] Dr. James Kennedy, *The Gates of Hell Shall Not Prevail*, p. 142

[131] Paul Fisher, *Behind the Lodge Door*, p. 244

[132] *Ibid.*

[133] Cited in *God and Government*, Vol. 1, p. 183

[134] J.M. O'Niell, *Religion and Education Under the Constitution*, p. 4

[135] Cited in *God and Government*, Vol. 1, p. 183

[136] Cited in *God and Government*, Vol. 2, p. xvii

[137] A.A. Hodge, *Evangelical Theology*, pp. 246-248

[138] Joseph Story, *Commentaries on the Constitution of the United States*, sections 1874, 1877

[139] R.J. Rushdoony, *Politics of Guilt and Pity*, p. 332

[140] Cited in *The Transformation*, p. 27

CHAPTER FIVE – AMERICA'S TROJAN HORSE: "PUBLIC" EDUCATION

[141] Cited in *The Unseen Hand* p. 385
[142] Dr. John Coleman, *One World Order: Socialist Dictatorship*, p. 69
[143] *Ibid.*
[144] B.K. Eakman, *The Cloning of the American Mind*, p 21
[145] *Ibid.*
[146] Harold Rugg, *The Great Technology*, p. 32 & 271
[147] Cited in *Education Reporter*, September, 2001, p. 3
[148] Paul Mantoux, Foreword to *International Understanding*, 1931.
[149] Cal Thomas, *The Things That Matter Most*, p. 161
[150] John Dunphy, *The Humanist*, Jan/Feb, 1983
[151] Johnny Esposito, *Temples of Darkness*, p. 87
[152] Cal Thomas, *The Things that Matter Most*, p. 39
[153] Charles Potter, *Humanism: A New Religion*, p. 128.
[154] Cited in *Education Reporter*, Number 182, p. 1
[155] National Commission on Excellence in Education, *A Nation at Risk*, 1983, p.5
[156] *Washington Times*, September 7, 1997, A1, A12
[157] Cited in *Education Reporter*, Number 182, p. 1
[158] Charlotte Thomson Iserbyt, *The Deliberate Dumbing Down of America*, p. 55
[159] Samuel Blumenfeld, *Is Public Education Necessary?*, p.
[160] Cited in *The Works of Thomas Jefferson*, (Vol. 1), p. 130
[161] Thomas Sowell, *Inside Public Education*, 121
[162] Thomas Sowell, *Inside Public Education*, p. 22
[163] *Ibid.*
[164] Madelyn Murray O'Hair, *Freedom Under Seige*.
[165] *The Review of the News*, (September, 10, 1980) , p. 37.
[166] Johnny Esposito, *Temples of Darkness*, p.
[167] Dobson and Bauer, *Children at Risk*, p. 35.
[168] Cited in *None Dare Call It Education*, p. viii.
[169] Cited in *Education Reporter*, Nebraska Senator Paul Hoagland to Everett Siliven's attorney in 1984
[170] Thomas Sowell, *Inside American Education*, p. 34
[171] Epperson, A. Ralph, *The Unseen Hand*, 287
[172] Cited in *Pavlov's Children*, p. ix
[173] Cited in *The Deliberate Dumbing Down of America*, p. 48.
[174] *Ibid.*, p. 81
[175] Jeri Lynn Ball, *Masters of Seduction*, p. 94, 96 & 112
[176] Cited in *Why Johnny Can't Tell Right from Wrong*, p. 80.
[177] Cited in *Pavlov's Children*, p. vii
[178] Cited in *USA Today*, Tuesday, Sept 10, 1991, "Schools are Undermining Parents' Values," p. 10A
[179] Cited in Video Presentation *Let My Children Go*
[180] Austin Sorenson, *Is America Committing Suicide?*, p. 75

CHAPTER SIX - A NATION DIVIDED: AMERICA'S SECOND CIVIL WAR

[181] Abraham Lincoln, "The Gettysburg Address," 1861
[182] Patrick J. Buchanan, The Death of the West, p. 7
[183] Cited in The Death of the West, p. 2
[184] Cited in The Death of the West, p. 2
[185] Patrick J. Buchanan, The Death of the West, p. 6
[186] Patrick J. Buchanan, The Death of the West, p. 2
[187] Patrick Buchanan, The Death of West, p. 7
[188] Robert Bork, Slouching Towards Gomorrah: Modern Liberalism and American Decline, p. 2
[189] Robert Bork, Slouching Towards Gomorrah: Modern Liberalism and American Decline, p. 6
[190] Robert Bork, Slouching Towards Gomorrah: Modern Liberalism and American Decline, p. 4
[191] Patrick J. Buchanan, The Death of the West, p. 8
[192] Cited in The Death of the West, p. 9
[193] Daniel Lapin, America's Real War, p.
[194] Cited in The Transformation, p. 32-33
[195] Patrick J. Buchanan, The Death of the West, p. 188
[196] Patrick J. Buchanan, The Death of the West, p. 188
[197] Patrick J. Buchanan, The Death of the West, p. 189
[198] Gary North, Cited in Christian Reconstruction; What It Is-What It Isn't, p. 40
[199] Patrick J. Buchanan, The Death of the West, p. 201
[200] Cited in The Death of the West, p. 201
[201] T.S. Eliot, Notes Toward the Defintion of Culture, p. 200
[202] Pat Buchanan, The Death of the West, p. 215
[203] Pat Buchanan, The Death of the West, p. 204
[204] Roger Kimball, The Long March, 274-275
[205] Kevin Swanson, The Second Mayflower, p. 10
[206] Kevin Swanson, The Second Mayflower, p. 10
[207] Kevin Swanson, The Second Mayflower, p. 16
[208] Kevin Swanson, The Second Mayflower, p. 42-43
[209] Dr. Sam Francis, Revolution from the Middle, 174
[210] Dr. Sam Francis, Revolution from the Middle, 174
[211] Daniel Lapin, America's Real War, p. 45
[212] Robert Bork, Slouching Towards Gomorrah: Modern Liberalism and American Decline, p. 7
[213] Dr. Henry Morris, When Christians Roamed the Earth, p. 11
[214] David A. Noebel, The Battle for Truth, p. viii
[215] Don Feder, A Jewish Conservative Looks at Pagan America, p. 10

CHAPTER SEVEN – CEASING TO BE GOOD

[216] Alexis de Tocqueville, *Democracy in America*, p.

[217] Alexis de Tocqueville, *Democracy in America*, p.

[218] Don Feder, *A Jewish Conservative Looks at Pagan America*, p. 11

[219] Don Feder, *A Jewish Conservative Looks at Pagan America*, p. 12

[220] Don Feder, *A Jewish Conservative Looks at Pagan America*, p. 10

[221] Kevin Swanson, *The Second Mayflower*, p. 8

[222] Ray Chamberlain, *Quotes and Quaint Stories of Great Americans*, p. 16

[223] "Issues 94" *1982 RAND Cooperation Study*, cited by Heritage Foundation, 35

[224] Kevin Swanson, *The Second Mayflower*, p. 8

[225] Patrick J. Buchanan, *The Death of the West*, p. 4-5

[226] Cited in *The Death of the West*, p. 5

[227] Patrick J. Buchanan, *The Death of the West*, p. 5

[228] Don Feder, *A Jewish Conservative Looks at Pagan America*, p. 12

[229] Des Griffin, *Fourth Reich of the Rich*, p. 9-10

[230] Cited in *Is America Committing Suicide?*, p. 81

[231] Cited in *Is America Committing Suicide?*, p. 82

[232] Cited in *Is America Committing Suicide?*, p. 84

[233] Cited in *Is America Committing Suicide?*, p. 82

[234] Joseph Farrah, "Happy Dependence Day," *WorldNETDaily*, July, 5, 2002

[235] Cited in *The Gates of Hell Shall Not Prevail*, p.

[236] Des Griffin, *Descent Into Slavery*, p. 2

[237] Jerome Carcopino, *Daily Life in Ancient Rome*, p. 78-79

[238] Jerome Carcopino, *Daily Life in Ancient Rome*, p. 79

[239] Jerome Carcopino, Daily Life in Ancient Rome, p. 90, 93 & 95

[240] Jerome Carcopino, Daily Life in Ancient Rome, p. 90, 93 & 95

[241] Philip Myers, *Rome: Its Rise And Fall*, p. 515 & 516

[242] Philip Myers, *Rome: Its Rise And Fall*, p. 515 & 516

[243] Jerome Carcopino, *Daily Life in Ancient Rome*, p.   238, 240 & 243

[244] Cited in *Is America Committing Suicide?*, p. 82

[245] Cited in *Citizen*, Focus on the Family, p.2

[246] Cited in *Impact*, "Pledge Ruling Shows Nation's Moral Decline," August 2002, p. 6

[247] Cited in *Impact*, "Pledge Ruling Shows Nation's Moral Decline," August 2002, p. 6

[248] Cited in *The Legal Alert*,

[249] Cited in *The Gates of Hell Shall Not Prevail*, p. 89

[250] Cited in *The Gates of Hell Shall Not Prevail*, p. 89

[251] Cited in *The Gates of Hell Shall Not Prevail*, p. 73

[252] Cited in *The Gates of Hell Shall Not Prevail*, p. 83

[253] Cited in the *Citizen*, Focus on the Family, p. 2

[254] George Barna, *Generation Next*, P. 38

[255] *Ibid.*

[256] *Ibid.*

[257] David T. Moore, *Five Lies of the Century*, p.66
[258] *Ibid.*
[259] *Ibid.*

CHAPTER EIGHT – AMERICAN HOLOCAUST

[260] Debra Rae, *The ABC's of Globalism*, p. 38
[261] Robert Bork, *Slouching Towards Gomorrah: Modern Liberalism and American Decline*, p. 173
[262] David James King, M.D., *Creating A Nation Under God.*,
[263] Cited in *The Rebirth of America*, p. 112
[264] Cited in *Is America Committing Suicide?*, p. 180
[265] Cited *The Rebirth of America*, p. 112
[266] David James King, *Creating A Nation Under God*, p. 170
[267] David James King, *Creating A Nation Under God*, p. 170-171
[268] Cited in *Is America Committing Suicide?*, p 185
[269] *Ibid.*
[270] *Ibid.*, 94-95
[271] Cited in *Is America Committing Suicide?*, p. 182
[272] Austin Sorenson, *Is America Committing Suicide?*, p. 182
[273] Cited in *Is America Committing Suicide?*, p. 184
[274] *Eternity*, October, 1973
[275] Debra Rae, *The ABC's of Globalism*, p. 39
[276] Debra Rae, *The ABC's of Globalism*, p. 39
[277] Alan Keyes, *Our Character , Our Nation*, p. 34
[278] Alan Keyes, *Our Character , Our Nation*, p. 34
[279] Alan Keyes, *Our Character , Our Nation*, p. 34
[280] Alan Keyes, *Our Character, Our Nation*, p. 34
[281] Cited in *The Transformation*, p. 94
[282] Cited in *The Transformation*, p. 89
[283] Tim LaHaye, *The Battle for the Mind*, p. 113
[284] Cited in *Is America Committing Suicide?*, p. 181
[285] Dr. Phil Stringer, *The Transformation*, p. 107
[286] Dr. Phil Stringer, *The Transformation*, p. 107
[287] Cited in *The Transformation*, p. 109-110.
[288] John McTernan, *God's Final Warning to America*, p. 134-135
[289] John McTernan, *God's Final Warning to America*, p.
[290] Cited in *Is America Committing Suicide?*, p. 182
[291] Cited in *Is America Committing Suicide?*, p. 183
[292] Cited in *Is America Committing Suicide?*, p. 184
[293] Dr. R.L. Hymers,Jr., *A Puritan Speaks to Our Dying Nation*, p. 6
[294] Cited in *Is America Committing Suicide?*, p. 184

CHAPTER NINE - HOMOSEXUALITY IN AMERICA

[295] Cited in *Is America Committing Suicide?*, p. 185
[296] Cited in *The Transformation*, p. 167
[297] Cited in *The Transformation*, p. 168
[298] David James King, M.D., *Creating A Nation Under God*, p. 157
[299] Alan Keyes, *Our Character, Our Nation*, p. 62
[300] *Ibid.*
[301] *Entertainment*, "Gay Hollywood 2000," A Special Report, p. 28
[302] *Entertainment*, "Gay Hollywood 2000," A Special Report, p. 26
[303] *Ibid.*
[304] *Ibid.*
[305] *Ibid.*
[306] *Ibid.*, 27-28
[307] *Ibid.*
[308] *Ibid.*
[309] *Ibid.*
[310] *Ibid.*
[311] *Ibid.*
[312] *Ibid.*
[313] *Ibid.* p. 158
[314] O.R. Adams, *As We Sodomize America*, p. 65
[315] O.R. Adams, *As We Sodomize America*, p. 67
[316] O.R. Adams, *As We Sodomize America*, p. 67
[317] Cited in *As We Sodomize America*, p. 67
[318] *Ibid.*
[319] O.R. Adams, *As We Sodomize America*, p. 70
[320] Cited in *As We Sodomize America*, p. 70
[321] Cited in *As We Sodomize America*, p. 69
[322] Cited in *As We Sodomize America*, p. 70
[323] Cited in *As We Sodomize America*, p. 70
[324] O.R. Adams, *As We Sodomize America*, p. 71
[325] O.R. Adams, *As We Sodomize America*, p. 72
[326] Alvin Toffler, *The Third Wave*, p. 212.
[327] Michealangelo Signorile (a leading homosexual writer), "Bridal Wave," Out, Dec/Jan, 1994, p. 161
[328] *The Washington Times*, "America is divided over homosexual adoption issue," p. 13
[329] *The Washington Times*, "America is divided over homosexual adoption issue," p. 13
[330] Cited in *The Second Mayflower*, p. 20
[331] Nebraska Medical Journal, 1985, Cited in *The Second Mayflower*, p. 20
[332] Cited in *The Second Mayflower*, p. 20
[333] Kevin Swanson, *The Second Mayflower*, p. 20
[334] Cited in *The Second Mayflower*, p. 20

[335] Kevin Swanson, *The Second Mayflower*, p. 20

[336] Judith A. Reisman, and Edward W. Eichel, *Kinsey, Sex and Fraud: The Indoctrination of a People*, p. 184

[337] Kathi Hudson, *Reinventing America's Schools, Vol. 1*, p. 70

[338] *Ibid.*, p. 108

[339] Cited in *As We Sodomize America*, p. 20-21

[340] Cited in *The Gates of Hell Shall Not Prevail*, p. 154

[341] Cited in *A Nation Adrift*, Video Presentation

[342] David James King, M.D., *Creating A Nation Under God*, p. 161

CHAPTER TEN - CLOUDS OF JUDGMENT ON THE HORIZON

[343] Des Griffin, *Midnight Messenger*, "Truth for Times Such As These," p. 21

[344] David Barton, *The Myth of Separation*, 217

[345] Cited in *Sodom Had No Bible*, p. 27

[346] Cited in *Sodom Had No Bible*, p. 27

[347] Cited in *Sodom Had No Bible*, p. 31

[348] Leonard Ravenhill, *Sodom Had No Bible*, p. 77

[349] Cited in *Is America Committing Suicide*, p. 231-232

[350] John Hagee, *Attack on America*, p.3

[351] *People Weekly*, September, 24, 2001

[352] *Newsweek*, September, 2001

[353] *People Weekly*, September, 2001

[354] John Hagee, *Attack on America*, p. 4

[355] Des Griffin, *Midnight Messenger*, "Truth for Times Such As These," p. 1

[356] Des Griffin, *Midnight Messenger*, "Truth for Times Such As These," p. 1

[357] John Hagee, *Attack on America*, p. 6

[358] John Hagee, *Attack on America*, p. 6

[359] Vance Havner, *Why Not Just Be Christians?* p. 89

[360] Joel Belz, *World*, November 24, 2001, p. 5

[361] Joel Belz, *World*, November 24, 2001, p. 5

[362] Joel Belz, *World*, November 24, 2001, p. 5

CHAPTER ELEVEN - IT'S TIME TO FIGHT

[363] Tim LaHaye, *Faith of our Founding Fathers*, p. 29

[364] Cited in *Is America Committing Suicide?*, p. 9

[365] Pat Buchanan, *The Death of the West*, p. 214

[366] Dr. Sam Francis, *Revolution from the Middle*, p. 174

[367] Dr. Sam Francis, *Revolution from the Middle*, p. 174

[368] John Stormer, *The Death of a Nation*, Dedication

[369] Charles Johnson, *One Hundred & One Famous Hymns*, p.87

[370] Cited in *Is America Committing Suicide?*, p. 9

[371] Cited in *America's God and Government,* p.

[372] Cited in *America's God and Country,* p. 235

[373] Cited in *The Gates of Hell Shall Not Prevail,* p. 218-219

[374] Austin Sorenson, *Is America Committing Suicide?,* p. 8

[375] Cited in *The Unseen Hand,* p. 435

To order the books
America at War or
Temples of Darkness
or to have Brother Esposito
speak to your
church or school,
or for more information
about *Pacific Publications*
contact us at
(562) 426-5214
EXT. 307